PHYSICIAN-ASSISTED DEATH

WHAT EVERYONE NEEDS TO KNOW®

PHYSICIAN-ASSISTED DEATH

WHAT EVERYONE NEEDS TO KNOW®

L. W. SUMNER

OXFORD
UNIVERSITY PRESS

Oxford University Press is a department of the University of Oxford. It furthers the University's objective of excellence in research, scholarship, and education by publishing worldwide. Oxford is a registered trademark of Oxford University Press in the UK and certain other countries.

"What Everyone Needs to Know" is a registered trademark of Oxford University Press.

Published in the United States of America by Oxford University Press 198 Madison Avenue, New York, NY 10016, United States of America.

© Oxford University Press 2017

CIP data is on file at the Library of Congress
ISBN 978-0-19-049017-1 (pbk); ISBN 978-0-19-049018-8 (hbk)

Hardback printed by Bridgeport National Bindery, Inc., United States of America

For David

CONTENTS

PREFACE

The 1994 US national elections do not particularly stand out in the memory. There was no presidential ballot since Bill Clinton was halfway through his first term (pre–Monica Lewinsky). True, the Republicans did seize the midterm momentum to achieve majorities in both the House and the Senate (in the former case, for the first time since the 1950s). But otherwise, not much of note seems to have happened. Except for one result in the Pacific Northwest, far from the center of national attention.

A political action group called Oregon Right to Die had collected enough signatures to get Measure 16—the Oregon Death with Dignity Act—onto the ballot. When it passed by a narrow margin of 51% to 49%, Oregon became the first US state, and one of the first jurisdictions in the world, to legalize any form of physician-assisted death. As a result of court challenges, the act did not come into effect until 1997, after it had been reaffirmed by a larger (60% to 40%) majority in another ballot initiative. But since that time terminally ill Oregonians have had the option of a physician-assisted death, an option that they have been exercising in ever-increasing numbers. Furthermore, the Death with Dignity Act has since served as the template for legalization in other states, by ballot initiative in Washington

(2008) and Colorado (2016) and by legislative action in Vermont (2013) and California (2015). The text of the act can be found in the Appendix to this book.

The movement that began in Oregon has put the issue of physician-assisted death firmly on the public agenda. Currently, bills aimed at legalizing the practice are under consideration in the legislatures of nearly half of the states. Intense public opinion battles between proponents and opponents are being fought across the country. The legalization movement is now spearheaded by Compassion and Choices, an advocacy organization based in Denver. The opposition consists largely of the Catholic Church, some evangelical denominations, and various right-to-life groups. The activity of these latter groups serves to remind us that abortion used to be the hottest of hot-button bioethical topics in this country. While that issue has hardly disappeared from public view—far from it—it has now been supplanted by physician-assisted death.

Why is the time now ripe for that debate? Public opinion surveys show that about 70% of Americans favor legalizing some form of physician-assisted death under some conditions, a figure that has risen considerably since the 1990s.[1] That increase in support is no doubt partly explained by a positive feedback loop. Since 1997 twelve jurisdictions, both domestic and foreign, have legalized some form of the practice. As more places take this step, it can come to seem more and more normal and legitimate, thereby driving up support in other places.

But there is more to it than that, and the more is largely demographic. On the one hand, the population of the United States is gradually aging, with a greater and greater percentage of people over the age of sixty-five. Currently, about 14% of Americans are in that age bracket, but this figure is projected to rise to over 20% by 2040.[2] It does not take rocket science to predict that more elderly people equals more people having to consider the timing and manner of their demise. In his 2014 book *Being Mortal* Atul Gawandi challenges his readers to ponder how they might want to live out the final stage of their lives on their own terms, including, where necessary, resistance to further medical interventions.[3] The book has remained on best-seller lists since its publication, reflecting a high degree of public interest in these matters.

But equally important is the fact that it is the baby boom generation who are now moving inexorably into old age. The oldest of them are about seventy now, the youngest around fifty-five. Furthermore, they are a generation who have been accustomed to being in control of the major decisions in their lives: where to go to school, what career path to pursue, whether to marry and/or have children, where to live, and so on. They have grown up with the expectation that they are the primary decision makers about their own health care as well: diet, exercise, birth control, immunization, and, should they need it, medical treatment. If they have managed their own treatment decisions up to the end-of-life stage, then it is inevitable that they will want to manage them through that period as well. To put it bluntly, they will want to have as many options available as possible in deciding how and when they will die. Physician-assisted death is one of those options; thus their increasing interest in having access to it, should they ever need it.

The aim of this book is to provide readers with the resources they will need in order to take up intelligent and informed positions in this important debate. It is a leaner, stripped-down version of my earlier book *Assisted Death.*[4] (Readers looking for the full scholarly treatment of the subject, complete with a lot more footnotes, are referred to that work.) The chapters that follow will explain and explore the principal ethical and legal issues concerning physician-assisted death. The ethical issues are all familiar ones. Do we have the right to determine when and how we will die? If so, by what means may we do so? Do we have the right to refuse further medical treatment, even if doing so will hasten our death? Is it permissible for doctors to administer high doses of opioids to control pain, even if doing so might hasten their patient's death? Is there an ethical difference between physician-assisted death and discontinuing life-sustaining treatment or administering terminal sedation? Is there an ethical difference between assisting a suicide and administering euthanasia? How is euthanasia different from murder? Do doctors have a duty not to kill their patients? Under what conditions, if any, can physician-assisted death be ethically justified?

The legal issues are equally familiar. Should assisting a suicide be a criminal offense? Should the law make exceptions to this prohibition? If so, under what circumstances and with what safeguards? Should the law make exceptions to the criminal prohibition of homicide to allow for voluntary euthanasia? If so, under what circumstances and with what safeguards? Is there a significant difference between legalizing assisted suicide and legalizing euthanasia? Could either of these practices find a place in standard hospice palliative care? How could abuses of the law be prevented? How could the slide down a slippery slope to ethically unacceptable practices be prevented? Is nonvoluntary euthanasia one of these practices? Could there be a case for legalizing it as well? What can we learn from jurisdictions in which one or more of these measures is legal?

The more argumentative chapters of the book are devoted to these ethical and legal questions: whether physician-assisted death can be ethically justified (Chapters 3 and 4) and whether it should be legally permitted (Chapters 7 and 8). To provide some valuable background for the legal arguments, Chapter 5 will outline the history of legalization, while Chapter 6 will describe the various possible types of legal regime. The two final chapters will set out some additional ethical and legal issues for future consideration (Chapter 9) and identify the ways in which legalization might be achieved (Chapter 10). But the book opens with two chapters whose aim is to explore some important questions about death itself (Chapter 1) and to situate the later ethical and legal discussions within the larger context of end-of-life care (Chapter 2).

PHYSICIAN-ASSISTED DEATH

WHAT EVERYONE NEEDS TO KNOW®

1

HOW SHOULD WE THINK ABOUT DEATH AND DYING?

How do we tell when death has occurred?

The answer to this question might seem straightforward: you are dead when you have stopped breathing and your heart has stopped beating. It's actually a little more complicated than that since both respiration and circulation can stop for a while and then be restarted, for instance, through cardiopulmonary resuscitation (CPR). So we need to sharpen our criterion for death a little more and say that death has occurred when these functions have irreversibly ceased. This, then, is the *cardiopulmonary criterion* for determining death, so named for its emphasis on heart and lung function. It was once our only criterion. If you came across, say, a drowning victim and wondered whether he or she might still be alive, you would check for a pulse and any sign of breathing, perhaps administer CPR, keep rechecking for vital signs, and then, finding none after a decent interval, declare that the person was dead.

The cardiopulmonary criterion served perfectly well for all practical purposes until the advent in the mid-twentieth century of mechanical ventilators capable of maintaining respiration after all brain functions had ceased. Formerly, when all brain functions had shut down as the result of catastrophic head injury, heart and lung functions would cease as well and death could be declared. Once ventilators became capable of performing the role of the brainstem in maintaining respiration (and therefore circulation) for patients in irreversible coma with no detectable brain activity, the question had to be faced whether such patients were alive or dead. The answer to this question was of obvious practical importance: to the health care team in making decisions about the patient's care, since once the patient has been declared dead no further medical treatment is appropriate, and to the patient's family, since death triggers various postmortem activities, such as mourning, cremation or burial, and transfer of property.

But it took on a further importance with the advent of widespread use of organs for transplant. An irreversibly comatose patient, maintained on a ventilator, could be an ideal source for such organs, but both ethics and law would condemn their removal while the patient was still alive. Since the cardiopulmonary criterion did not distinguish between spontaneous and artificially maintained respiratory function, it became imperative for medical practitioners, hospitals, and governments to develop a less ambiguous criterion for patients in irreversible coma. A significant step toward this goal was taken in 1968 when a special committee at the Harvard Medical School defined *irreversible coma* as the permanent loss of all brain functions—right down to the most primitive brainstem functions—and proposed procedures for diagnosing the condition.[1] More to our present purpose, it also proposed that physicians use these procedures in determining death, thereby endorsing the *whole-brain criterion*: death has occurred when all brain functions, including brainstem functions, have irreversibly ceased.

The whole-brain criterion was intended by its advocates as a disambiguation, rather than a revision, of the former emphasis on heart–lung function. In their view the cardiopulmonary criterion had always implicitly assumed that

persons should be declared dead when they had irreversibly lost the capacity to breathe and circulate blood on their
own, without mechanical assistance. Since patients in irreversible coma were incapable of supporting their own circulation and respiration, even under the old criterion they
could be declared dead.

By the 1990s most jurisdictions had adopted the whole-
brain criterion as the clinical and legal standard for determining death. However, from the outset it has not been
without its critics. Some have contended that it does not
go far enough. Just as the condition of irreversible coma
forced a rethinking of the traditional cardiopulmonary
criterion once artificial means of maintaining respiration
became available, so, the critics argued, the condition of
permanent vegetative state (PVS) should force a rethinking of the whole-brain criterion. PVS differs from coma in
that while all "higher-brain" functions (those supported
by the cerebrum and especially the cortex) have ceased,
"lower-brain" (and especially brainstem) functions are still
intact. These differential outcomes can occur because the
cerebrum is more sensitive than the brainstem to interrup-
tions of circulation; a cutoff of oxygen supply to the brain
of several minutes' duration might damage the cerebrum
beyond repair while allowing the brainstem to resume
functioning once circulation has been restored.

Like coma patients, PVS patients lack all capacity for
cognitive functions, external awareness, and purposeful
movement. However, unlike coma patients, their eyes are
open, they are capable of reflex movements (such as blinking and swallowing), and they have sleep–wake cycles.
More important for present purposes, they are usually
capable of breathing on their own, without mechanical
assistance. As a result, according to the whole-brain criterion, they are alive. Some commentators, however, have
argued that since consciousness is irreversibly lost in both

cases, the distinction that this criterion draws between co-matose patients and PVS patients is arbitrary. They have instead advocated a *higher-brain criterion* for determining death: death has occurred when all higher-brain functions have irreversibly ceased. Everyone declared dead by the whole-brain criterion will also be declared dead by this cri-terion but not vice versa (as we have seen for PVS patients). In this respect, the whole-brain criterion is more conserva-tive; while the higher-brain alternative continues to have its philosophical defenders, it has yet to be adopted by any legal jurisdiction.

More recently, some traditionalists have advocated a reinstatement of the old cardiopulmonary criterion. They agree with the higher-brain advocates that any line drawn between irreversible coma and PVS is arbitrary, but they contend that both categories of patients should be deemed to be alive. Their principal argument is that there are many organic functions being carried out within the bodies of coma patients, despite their inability to breathe on their own. These functions include the exchange of oxygen and carbon dioxide, nutrition at the cellular level, homeostasis, elimination of cellular wastes, maintenance of body tem-perature, wound healing, and fighting of infection. When coma patients display so many signs of self-maintained organic functioning, the argument goes, it is unwarranted to declare them dead just because their breathing must be mechanically assisted. If respiration and circulation con-tinue (and continue to support all of these further func-tions), then it should not matter whether they are sponta-neous; the patient is alive in either case.

What do we mean by death?

There remains therefore a lively debate over the adequacy of the whole-brain criterion, despite its establishment as clinical and legal orthodoxy, a debate that reflects a deeper philosophical divide over the concept of death. Thus far we have been discussing various operational criteria for determining death whose function is to suggest procedures and tests for ascertaining whether (and when) someone has died. They are not different concepts, or definitions, of death. The function of a concept—or a conceptual analysis—of death is to reveal its nature: to tell us what it is, not just when it occurs. Though a criterion is not a concept, different criteria for determining death may presuppose, or cohere with, different concepts of death. Put another way, the concept of death you have in mind may determine what will seem to you intuitively plausible as a criterion. So let us now turn from criteria to concepts.

It seems safe to say that death is the end of life—safe but also unilluminating because it simply invites the further question: What is life? We can perhaps take a small step forward by requiring that an adequate account of the life (and death) of a thing rest on or reflect an adequate account of the nature of that thing. Since we are primarily interested in *our* death, that raises the question of how we are to understand our nature. Philosophers have tended to provide two different (though not mutually exclusive) answers to this question: we are animals (or, more broadly, organisms) and we are persons. As the former, we share a nature with all other animals (or all other organisms), so it seems plausible to suppose that the best account of our death will apply to all of them as well. As the latter, we may be unique, or we may share a nature with a relatively small set of other highly developed animals (depending on how the notion of a person is understood), and in that case we should expect the best account for us to be (more or less) species-specific. In any case, it looks as though there should be two quite different concepts of death that pertain to us, one for organisms and one for persons.

We might call the former concept *biological death*. We can work toward it by beginning with the assumption that the life of an organism consists of the integrated functioning of its several subsystems that are working together in a coordinated fashion so as to support the functioning of the organism as a whole. The particular subsystems in question will vary with the type of organism; in higher animals like us they will include the respiratory, circulatory, excretory, endocrine, homeostatic, immune, and reproductive. It would follow that the death of an organism would consist in the irreversible cessation of this integrated functioning. This concept of biological death has the advantage of being equally applicable to all living things; in this concept the death of a human is the same as the death of a frog or a tree or a bacterium (though, of course, the precise criteria for determining death will be species-specific). It seems to be what we usually have in mind when saying that someone has died: the person is no longer breathing, the heart has stopped, the body is beginning to get cold and stiff, and eventually it starts to decompose. The biological concept also seems to be the one presupposed by the cardiopulmonary criterion, which purports to provide the appropriate means of determining death for the particular organisms that we are.

But we are not just organisms: we are also persons. What is required in order to count as a person has been much debated by philosophers, and the requirements have included such features as consciousness, self-consciousness, memory, language use, rationality, and the capacity to construct a life narrative. We need not settle this issue here since it is clear that all of these features require a sophisticated mind (and therefore a complex brain capable of supporting such a mind). The concept of a person is therefore not bodily but psychological, and the end of a person would therefore be marked by the irreversible cessation of whatever psychological states or capacities are taken to be essential to being a person. Let us call this *personal death*. Normally we should expect it to coincide with biological death: if the integrated functioning of the body ceases, then the functioning of the brain will also cease, and since the brain is the substrate of the psychological states that constitute a person, the person will cease as well. But we now know that while biological death is sufficient for personal death (barring a disembodied "afterlife"), it is not necessary. PVS patients are not biologically dead since their bodies remain capable of integrated functioning, but they have permanently lost all capacity for consciousness, which would seem to be the minimum requirement for being a person. In these cases, therefore, personal death has preceded biological death. As the result of oxygen deprivation caused by an auto accident, Nancy Cruzan lapsed into PVS in January 1983, and the integrated functioning of her body ceased in December 1990 after her feeding tube was removed. Her personal death and her biological death were therefore nearly eight years apart. Nancy's family appeared to recognize both aspects of her death by inscribing on her grave marker "DEPARTED Jan 11, 1983/AT PEACE Dec 26, 1990." Because the higher-brain criterion yields the result that PVS patients are dead, it would seem to track the concept of personal, rather than biological, death.

So we seem to have two concepts of death: biological and personal. And our criteria for determining death seem to line up as follows: the cardiopulmonary criterion appears to presuppose biological death, while the higher-brain alternative appears to be appropriate for personal death. It is an interesting, and important, result of this analysis that these pairings seem to leave no room for the whole-brain criterion, despite its near-universal adoption as the clinical and legal standard for determining death. It is not a good fit with the personal concept of death since, while the cessation of all brain functions is sufficient for personal death, it is not necessary (as in PVS cases). But it is not a good fit with the biological concept either if, as its critics contend, many integrative bodily functions can survive the loss of all brain function.

Because biological and personal death normally coincide, the cardiopulmonary and higher-brain criteria will normally yield the same results. But when they diverge, as in PVS cases, which concept and which criterion should we prefer? The answer to that question is surely context-specific; it is, for instance, easy to imagine oneself in the position of Nancy Cruzan's parents when they take the view that they lost their daughter in 1983, not 1990. However, for clinical practice the higher-brain criterion yields the desperately counterintuitive result that Nancy was dead throughout those eight years when she was breathing on her own, her heart was beating, her eyes were open, and she was blinking and swallowing. These are not things that corpses do, and it seems too much to ask clinical staff to see Nancy, and other PVS patients, as dead. (It may be hard enough for clinical staff to see even irreversibly comatose patients as dead, as evidenced by the fact that disconnecting the ventilator is commonly characterized as "the removal of life support.")

It is also preposterous to suggest that normal postmortem activities (such as burial or cremation) could have been initiated while Nancy was still breathing, rather than waiting for her biological death. In dealing with the difficult ethical and legal issues concerning the withdrawal of life-sustaining treatment (especially nutrition and hydration) from PVS patients like Nancy Cruzan and, more recently, Terri Schiavo, no court has ever taken the position that these patients are already dead. PVS cases therefore strongly suggest that the higher-brain criterion is misconceived as a means of determining death. It may fare much better if it is taken to mark not the end of life but the end of everything that is valuable or worthwhile in life. In that case it would still point to something important in the timeline of a life, even if it is not the transition from being alive to being dead.

Why is it (usually) a bad thing to die?

We normally assume that death, especially premature death, is one of the worst misfortunes that can befall us. We fear and dread our own death and, if necessary, take elaborate precautions to avoid it. If we suffer a life-threatening illness or injury, we want the best care available in order to fend off the Grim Reaper. The worst-case scenario we can imagine is that moment in the doctor's office when we are told that there is nothing else that can be done and that death is imminent. We grieve and mourn the deaths of those close to us, not just for our loss of them but also for what they have lost. We find the deaths of others particularly unfortunate or tragic when they are struck down in their youth or in the prime of life, before they have been able to realize their life's full potential. Many of us take comfort in religious belief, which holds out the promise of an "afterlife," thereby effectively denying the reality of death. Finally, the law treats homicide as the gravest of offenses against the person, presumably because it judges the harm it inflicts on the victim to be of a special seriousness.

And yet it can be surprisingly difficult to explain why it is such a bad thing to die. Most of the evils in life are events or conditions that we experience or live through. The clearest case, of course, is physical suffering, but there are many others: depression, anxiety, frustration, disappointment, humiliation, loneliness, the loss of loved ones, a sense of injustice or betrayal. What all of these conditions have in common is that we experience them as *intrinsically* bad—that is, they are bad (for us) just in themselves and quite apart from anything else to which they might lead or with which they might be connected. But if, as seems to be the case, death is the absence of all experience, then being dead seems to preclude all of these evils. Unless we presuppose an afterlife, the dead seem to be beyond being harmed. If nothing bad can happen to us once we are dead, then how can dying be bad for us?

Some philosophers, especially those in the Epicurean tradition, draw the conclusion that it cannot. The Roman philosopher Lucretius put the point thus:

> Death therefore to us is nothing, concerns us not a jot.... For he whom evil is to befall, must in his own person exist at the very time it comes, if the misery and suffering are haply to have any place at all; but since death precludes this, and forbids him to be, upon whom the ills can be brought, you may be sure that we have nothing to fear after death, and that he who exists not, cannot become miserable.[2]

Unfortunately, there is an obvious flaw in this comforting line of thought. If all of the intrinsic evils in life are experienced, then so are all of the intrinsic goods: pleasure, enjoyment, happiness, love, a sense of accomplishment or success, peace of mind, wisdom. It follows that if being dead precludes all of the experiential evils, it equally wipes out all of the experiential goods. From this vantage point, being dead doesn't seem like such a good thing after all.

The key to understanding the badness of death lies in recognizing that not all goods (or evils) are intrinsic in this way. Things can also be good or bad for us *extrinsically*— that is, by virtue of the events or conditions that they bring about or to which they are connected. The classic example of an extrinsic good is money: we seek and value it not primarily for its own sake but for the good things in life that it enables us to acquire. The same may be true of education, job training, or regular workouts at the gym. On the negative side, most losses are extrinsic evils: the badness of the loss consists in whatever (intrinsically) good things one thereby misses out on.

This suggests a fairly obvious way of thinking about the badness of death. It is a commonplace that death is the loss of life. But then it is a natural further thought that the disvalue of death lies in the value of the life thereby lost. This is the *deprivation account* of the badness of death: death is (extrinsically) bad for us by virtue of depriving us of the (intrinsic) goods of continued life. On this account showing that dying now would be bad for you requires a comparison between two possible outcomes: the one in which you die now and the one in which you live on. Doubtless most stages of your life contain a mix of intrinsic goods and intrinsic evils. But if the goods outweigh the evils over a particular stage of your life, then that life stage is overall (on balance) good for you or worth living. So suppose that the life you would have from now on would be (on balance) good for you until it reaches its terminus at some later time. In that case it would be better for you to continue living than to die now, and death therefore would be bad for you (since it would deprive you of this good future).

How might death sometimes be a good thing?

The deprivation account captures most people's intuitive thinking about the badness of death. On this account the (extrinsic) disvalue of death depends on the (intrinsic) value of the (further) life foregone. It would seem to follow then that how bad your death is for you will depend on how much value there would have been in your continued life. But now we need to note an important implication of the deprivation account for the end-of-life issues we will be discussing. If death is (extrinsically) bad when it deprives you of a continued good life, then it follows that it can be (extrinsically) good when it saves you from a continued bad one (a life, let us say, that would be full of unavoidable suffering). On the deprivation account death is not always harmful or something to be feared; it can be beneficial or something to be embraced. Whether it harms or benefits depends on the circumstances of your life—and, in particular, on the expected quality (and duration) of your continued life. If your prospects are sufficiently bleak, then death can be a welcome release.

Since we are all going to die sooner or later, the practical question is not whether to die but rather when and how. What the deprivation account suggests is that it can sometimes be beneficial to die sooner rather than later, if what is thereby avoided is just prolonged suffering. This can be the case for some people with serious illnesses, such as cancer, that have progressed to the point where effective treatment has become impossible and are accompanied by physical and psychological symptoms that are experienced as distressing or even unbearable. In that case being able to hasten death may also have the benefit of being able to manage its circumstances—such as time, place, and the company of loved ones—rather than leaving these to be dictated by the illness.

If so, then the further questions become how death might be hastened, whether it would be ethical to do so, and whether it should be legal to do so. Those are the main questions of this book. But before we turn to them, let's take a reality check on the current American way of death.

How and where do we typically die?

Suppose, for the sake of argument, that you are currently in your mid-forties. Then you can look forward, on average, to about thirty-six more years of life (slightly less if you are male, slightly more if you are female). You have about a 50% chance of succumbing eventually to one of the two major killers: heart disease or cancer. If you manage to dodge both of those bullets, then your end is likely to be due either to some other disease (respiratory, cerebro-vascular, Alzheimer's, diabetes, etc.) or to some traumatic event such as accident or suicide.[3]

What you eventually die of has implications for where you are likely to die. If your end is violent, then chances are that it will also be sudden, with little or no time spent in a health care institution. But if you die of any of the aforementioned illnesses, then you are likely to find yourself with an extended stay in a hospital, nursing home, or hospice. Studies have shown that about 80% of Americans want to die at home. But about 60% of deaths currently occur in hospitals and another 20% in other institutions.[4] Only a minority of Americans therefore manage to die in the home setting that most of them say they would prefer.

The major disease killers have another important implication: most of them take a while to finish you off. If you fall prey to one of them, then your health is likely to follow a downward trajectory, during the latter stages of which you will be receiving pretty intensive treatment by a health care team (probably in an institution but possibly at home). Should you reach that stage, then at least for a while you will probably have both the ability and the opportunity to play an active part in your own medical decisions. You may need to decide whether to undertake aggressive treatment of your condition, through such means as surgery or chemotherapy. Or, having commenced such treatment, you may at some point need to decide whether it is worth continuing or, instead, whether it might be time to shift into managing your symptoms by means of palliative or hospice care. As well as declining any further active treatment, you might decide to refuse antibiotics in case of infection or CPR in case of cardiac arrest. This might be the time to write, or rewrite, an advance directive informing your substitute decision maker of your treatment (or nontreatment) wishes should you become unable to decide for yourself. Should your physical symptoms become too much to bear toward the end, you might be offered palliative sedation that would render you unconscious until your death.

All of the foregoing options will probably be available to you wherever you happen to live—and die. But this final stage of your life may also be the time when, should it be legal in your jurisdiction, you will think about requesting a physician-assisted death. Whether you should also have that option is the subject of this book.

2

WHAT IS END-OF-LIFE CARE?

What is the end of life?

The short answer to this question is pretty obvious: death. But we can be a little more relaxed about it. Patients who die of chronic diseases such as cancer usually enter a phase in the latter stages of their illness during which the likelihood and proximity of death start to become more evident. We could say that this happens when it becomes reasonable to anticipate that, even with continued active treatment of the illness, death is likely to occur in the near future. This is still rather vague, but it is difficult to make it more precise without imposing an arbitrary timeline. One criterion often used is that death is anticipated within six months (this is a qualification in most American jurisdictions for admission to a hospice). That timeline may fit most cases quite well, but it does not work for all. Some degenerative conditions, such as amyotrophic lateral sclerosis (ALS) and Alzheimer's disease, are terminal but are marked by a more extended decline toward death. People with such a condition could well be regarded, and could well regard themselves, as being at the end of life though they have well over six months to go.

So we will have to be content with the vagueness of the notion of the end of life, at least as far as a timeline is concerned. It is better to think of it in functional, rather than temporal, terms. The end-of-life phase has been reached when care planning needs to start taking into account not just the active treatment of the illness in question, which may continue, but also how to ensure that the eventual dying process goes as well for the patient as it can. End-of-life care, then, is care that is oriented toward preparing for death as well as prolonging life. Often, it will involve the initiation of some form of palliative care, either alongside active treatment or when such treatment has finally been abandoned. The World Health Organization defines *palliative care* as "an approach that improves the quality of life of patients (adults and children) and their families who are facing problems associated with life-threatening illness. It prevents and relieves suffering through the early identification, correct assessment and treatment of pain and other problems, whether physical, psychosocial or spiritual."[1] Palliative care may be delivered in an institution—a hospital, long-term care facility, or hospice—or at home and may be provided by specialists or by a family physician. Wherever and however it is provided, its emphasis is on symptom control and on ensuring the conditions for a "good death."

What end-of-life treatment options are currently available to patients?

The easiest way to lay out the possible courses of treatment is to follow the narrative of an imaginary cancer patient we will call Rebecca: a fifty-three-year-old successful businesswoman with a loving husband and a devoted daughter in her early twenties. Rebecca has been diagnosed with an aggressive tumor in her colon, which has metastasized first into her bloodstream and lymph channels and then into her liver. When she asks for a prognosis she is told by her oncologist that the five-year survival rate for patients with her condition is about 10%, even with active treatment. She is offered chemotherapy, which is the standard treatment for her cancer. Even with it her chances of long-term survival are slim, but if left untreated, the disease will almost certainly kill her within the next few months. This is Rebecca's first decision point: Does she commence treatment?

In making her decision Rebecca takes into consideration a number of factors: her relatively young age, her family, the predictable side effects of the treatment, and the likelihood that it will significantly extend her life. Somewhat against her better judgment but in order to calm the anxieties of her family, Rebecca agrees to a round of chemotherapy. Unfortunately, this has to be soon terminated when she develops high fevers and constipation alternating with diarrhea. At this point Rebecca decides to forgo any further chemotherapy. In doing so she is exercising one of the end-of-life options available to her: she is refusing further active treatment of her cancer. No chemotherapy, no surgery, no radiation: nothing that might have any effect in slowing, or even stopping, the progress of her disease. As her condition worsens she may later decide to decline other forms of treatment that might prolong her life, including cardiopulmonary resuscitation or even antibiotics to fight infection.

Unfortunately, Rebecca's condition does worsen quite rapidly. Soon, narcotics are necessary to deal with the pain caused by the growing liver metastases. A massive tumor develops in her pelvis, and her legs become swollen when pressure from the tumor prevents the veins from draining fluid from them. She is admitted to a hospice with nausea, vomiting, diarrhea, high fever, and pain from the liver and pelvic tumors. At this point Rebecca has transitioned into palliative care, with its focus on symptom relief. Various pharmacological means are available to combat her symptoms, but the main effort focuses on her pain, for which she is administered ever-increasing doses of opioids.

Her physician tells her that she has at most a few weeks left before she succumbs to the cancer, during which time these symptoms will grow worse. While medication can control much of the pain she will experience, it cannot eliminate all of it, and there is little that can be done to alleviate the other symptoms. When the opioids prove insufficient to reduce the pain to a tolerable level, she is offered sedatives, such as barbiturates or benzodiazepines, that can be titrated to achieve or maintain differing levels of diminished consciousness, ranging from drowsiness to deep sleep. Where complete unconsciousness is the intended effect, it can be either intermittent—where the patient is brought back to wakefulness from time to time—or continuous. When the unconsciousness is deep and maintained continuously to the point of death, it is common to label it *palliative sedation* or, more graphically, *terminal sedation*. Should Rebecca elect this means of symptom control, she will almost certainly also refuse artificial nutrition and hydration for the period of sedation.

So far, then, we have identified three end-of-life treatment options that are available to patients in Rebecca's rather dire circumstances: refusal of (further) active treatment, administration of high doses of opioids for pain management, and terminal sedation. Each of these will be explored in more detail in the next few sections. Of course, Rebecca might have a fourth option available as well should she happen to live in a jurisdiction that has legalized physician-assisted death. We will come to this option after discussing the other three.

Do patients have the right to refuse treatment?

In order to understand a patient's right to refuse treatment, we must first attend to one of the cornerstones of biomedical ethics: the doctrine of informed consent. The basic idea behind the doctrine is that it is permissible for a health care provider to administer medical treatment to a patient only with the consent of the patient. More particularly, under the doctrine four conditions must be satisfied in order for medical treatment to be justified:

Consent. The relevant decision maker concerning the treatment must agree to it. This agreement must be quite specific: consent for *this* treatment to be administered on *this* occasion by *this* provider. Normally, the relevant decision maker will be the patient himself or herself. But when the patient is a minor or is in some way incapacitated, it may be another agent empowered to make decisions on the patient's behalf. For now we will assume that consent is being sought from, and given by, the patient; decisions by substitute decision makers will be discussed later (in Chapter 9). The patient may take the initiative by actively requesting the treatment or, alternatively, may agree to it once it has been suggested or proposed by the provider.

Capacity. The patient must be decisionally capable at the time with respect to the treatment options in question. *Decisional capacity* (or *competence*) is basically the ability to make a reasoned decision whether to accept or reject a particular form of treatment. At a minimum it includes the ability to understand and appreciate the nature and consequences of both agreeing to and declining a treatment option. Decisional capacity is the default presumption for adult patients. However, the presumption is rebuttable by evidence of some standing mental illness or disability serious enough to impair cognitive functioning. Alternatively, the impairment may be temporary and situational, when thinking is disordered by factors such as severe trauma, alcohol or drug intoxication, or hysteria. Young children, on the other hand, will be presumed to be decisionally incapable, though there will, of course, be a gray area located somewhere during adolescence (so-called mature minors). It is important to note that the relevant decisional capacity for informed consent to treatment is the ability to make a reasoned decision concerning *this* treatment at *this* time. A person may be competent to make other personal decisions (such as financial ones) but not treatment decisions, may be competent to make some treatment decisions but not others, or may be competent to make particular treatment decisions at some times and not others.

Voluntariness. The patient's consent must be free of undue influence and coercion, whether by providers or by family or friends. It is recognized, of course, that our decision-making as patients will often be influenced by what others think or suggest or by our knowledge of what they want or would prefer. Since it would aim much too high to purge decision-making of all such influences, the issue of voluntariness will turn on when such influences are "undue"—that is, when they rise to the level of "force, fraud, deceit, duress, overreaching, or other ulterior form of constraint or coercion."[2] As with decisional capacity, there will inevitably be borderline cases in which the voluntariness of patient consent to treatment is uncertain.

Disclosure. The patient must be provided with adequate information concerning the treatment option in question. This information will normally include the patient's diagnosis, prognosis in the absence of treatment (including any uncertainty attending either of these matters), the nature of each of the available treatment options, the probable outcome of each option, and the risks attached to each option. The general rule for disclosure is that it should include all of the information that a reasonable person in this particular patient's circumstances would need in order to make a reasoned decision concerning the treatment in question. In order to facilitate this decision-making, the information must therefore be communicated in a manner that the patient is capable of comprehending.

So formulated, the doctrine of informed consent puts a decisionally capable patient in the driver's seat with respect to medical treatment: no treatment may be initiated, or continued, without the patient's free and informed consent. However, like most ethical rules, the doctrine does admit of some exceptions. One of these exceptions concerns emergencies in which treatment is urgently needed in order to prevent serious harm, the patient is so incapacitated by the condition that he or she is unable to give consent, and no substitute decision maker is at hand. Under these circumstances patient consent may be presumed, on the assumption that a reasonable person in this situation would agree to treatment, or the treatment may be justified on grounds of necessity as being in the patient's best interest. It is worth distinguishing these emergency situations, in which patient incapacity may be temporary, from cases of permanent incapacity, in which consent must be sought from substitute decision makers. In the emergency situation the physician may be answerable to the patient once capacity has been regained.

In other cases the interests of third parties, or society at large, may justify treatment without the consent, or even despite the refusal, of a decisionally capable patient. For instance, someone carrying an infectious disease may be subjected to compulsory quarantine, examination, and blood sampling in order to protect others against the spread of the infection, or a decisionally capable person with mental health problems may be subjected to involuntary confinement if found to be a danger to others. There are, however, limits to the "harm to others" exception: a parent, even if a good match, cannot be compelled to donate a kidney, or even blood, to a child in need of it.

So far we have traced the main elements of the doctrine of informed consent. But it is also instructive to seek its ethical justification. Since the primary purpose of the doctrine is to protect patients from unwanted treatment, we should expect its justification to be grounded in the patient values that it thereby safeguards or promotes. Two such values seem particularly pertinent: autonomy (or self-determination) and well-being. Of the two, the former is the more intuitively obvious. Exercising autonomy or self-determination is a matter of managing one's life in accordance with one's own values and priorities. It therefore requires being the one who makes the major decisions about how that life is to go: what educational and career path to pursue, where to live, whether and whom to marry, whether to have children, how to spend leisure time, what social/political causes to support, and so on. The presumptive point of the requirement of informed consent is to provide us with the same managerial opportunity with respect to our health care. While many treatment decisions will be relatively trivial, some will have a profound impact on the course of our lives. In theory at least, the regime of informed consent is meant to ensure that no treatment goes forward unless or until we have signed off on it. No one else gets to make that final decision, no one else gets to determine how our therapeutic process will go—only we do.

However, autonomy is clearly not the only value in play. While self-determination may be valuable in its own right—most of us want to be masters of our fate and captains of our souls—it is also an effective means whereby we are enabled to pursue our own well-being. A decisionally capable and well-informed agent is normally in a better position to act in his or her best interest than is any third party. This is especially so if well-being is interpreted subjectively so that what is best for a person is ultimately determined by his or her own tastes, preferences, and values. In that case, the goals that an agent freely chooses to pursue will normally coincide with, or constitute, his or her well-being. Giving the agent final authority over health care decisions will then be an effective way of ensuring that those decisions are guided by his or her own conception of what is good and not by someone else's.

Autonomy and well-being will normally run together as the justifying values of the doctrine of informed consent. Normally, but not necessarily. Free and fully informed self-determiners who surpass the threshold of decisional capability are nonetheless capable of making decisions to their own detriment. This can happen because they have goals other than their own self-interest and may choose what is worse for themselves because it will be better for others. But it can also happen if their decision-making processes are distorted by self-deception, denial, phobias, traumatic memories, and the like. In cases like these the twin justifying values of the doctrine come apart: respecting autonomy will require acquiescence to the patient's decision, while promoting health and well-being will urge disregarding it. In these cases the doctrine tends to side with autonomy against well-being: as long as the patient in question is decisionally capable, fully informed, and free of the undue influence of others, in the absence of consent no treatment may be administered, whatever the adverse impact of nontreatment might be.

In other respects, however, well-being may compete more successfully with self-determination. Emergency situations may be viewed as those in which the immediate interests of the patient override the consent requirement;

at any rate, to presume patient consent in such cases is to presume that, if consulted, the patient would agree to the course of action necessary to prevent grave harm or loss of life, that is, the course of action that would be best for him or her. Finally, when treatment can be compelled to protect others, autonomy is clearly subordinated to well-being, albeit not that of the patient.

Once the requirement of informed consent is in place, the right of decisionally capable patients to refuse treatment follows as a simple matter of logic: if patient consent is necessary for treatment to be justified, then patient refusal of consent is sufficient for it to be unjustified. Besides decisional capacity, we may assume that the further conditions of voluntariness and disclosure also apply to refusal just as they do to consent so that we are speaking here of patients' free and informed refusal of medical treatment. That leaves us with only two questions worthy of discussion: Do matters stand differently if the treatment in question is necessary in order to sustain life? And what counts, in this context, as life-sustaining medical treatment?

Do patients have the right to refuse life-sustaining treatment?

While much medical treatment is routine, some is not. At the extreme, when initiation or continuation of treatment is necessary in order to sustain life, refusal of treatment becomes life-threatening. Even in these cases there is no real ethical or legal issue about the patient's right of refusal. It is well established in both ethics and law that even when the stakes are this high the free and informed refusal of treatment by a decisionally capable patient must be respected. This is not the end of the story, however, since there is another way, short of overriding patient refusal, in which the higher stakes in life-and-death situations may be taken into account. Some bioethicists have proposed a sliding scale for determinations of decisional capacity.[3] For routine, low-risk medical interventions, the capacity threshold could be set at a correspondingly low level, one that is comparatively easy for patients to surpass, while in the case of treatment necessary to prolong life, in which the risk is the probability—or even certainty—of death, the threshold would be higher.

This may be seen as a way of balancing the two fundamental values served by informed consent: patient autonomy and patient well-being. When the stakes are raised for the latter, a correspondingly higher standard will be applied to the former in order to provide additional assurance that authority over the decision should properly be left in the hands of the patient. The effect of raising the threshold for decisional capacity is therefore to introduce a little more paternalism into the decision-making process: a higher protection of well-being at some cost to autonomy. But it remains the case that treatment decisions made by patients who surpass the higher threshold must be respected, whatever the cost to their well-being.

The idea of a sliding scale for decisional capacity enjoys a good deal of common-sense support. Parents will generally allow a young child some decisional authority over low-risk matters (what color clothes to wear) but not high-risk ones (whether to play in the street). For the latter they will wait until the child is older and better able to appreciate the consequences of his or her actions. Applying the sliding-scale approach to medical decision-making will sometimes have the result of imposing a higher standard of capacity for refusal of a particular treatment than for consent to the very same treatment—in cases, for instance, in which the treatment in question would clearly be beneficial and its omission would equally clearly be life-threatening. But this does not seem anomalous since the aim is to ensure that self-determination is most fully engaged when the consequences for well-being are most serious—and especially if they are irreversible.

One way to operationalize such a sliding scale would be to adopt a variable age of consent to (or refusal of) treatment. A fourteen-year-old girl might, for instance, be deemed decisionally capable with respect to relatively low-risk decisions (whether to use contraception or seek an abortion) but not high-risk ones (whether to embark on a round of chemotherapy for leukemia or continue renal dialysis). In general, younger adolescents who are capable of understanding the nature of the treatment in question and the consequences of accepting or rejecting it might meet the standard of decisional capacity for a broad range of treatment decisions but not those in which either the acceptance or the rejection of the treatment carries with it a serious risk to life. For those decisions the bar might be raised higher so as to require either parental endorsement of the decision or some independent evidence that it is in the patient's best interest.

Another sliding scale for decisional capacity might concern the absence of distorting factors, such as mental illness or depression, which are known to impair judgment. When life-sustaining treatment is being refused it might sometimes be advisable to refer a patient for psychological or psychiatric examination if there is some initial suspicion that such factors are affecting his or her decision-making, whereas no similar referral would be appropriate for more routine decisions. We might similarly raise the bar for patients who are cognitively impaired, deeming them decisionally capable with respect to relatively minor therapeutic interventions but not life-or-death decisions.

The same sliding-scale idea can readily be applied to the other conditions of valid consent or refusal as well. When death is the expected outcome of treatment refusal it may be important to have a documentary record of the patient's decision—such as a signed refusal form. It would also seem appropriate to put in place a more rigorous procedure for ensuring that the patient's decision is fully voluntary and free of the undue influence of others and that it represents the patient's stable and enduring wishes. This might be accomplished by interviewing the patient and family, by offering counseling, or, where appropriate, by asking the patient to reaffirm the decision over a suitable period of time. A more rigorous standard of disclosure might also be required when life is at stake in order to ensure that the patient fully understands the consequences of the decision. The effect of all of these higher standards—for consent, capacity, voluntariness, and disclosure—is to introduce additional safeguards of patient well-being when life is at risk because life-sustaining treatment is being refused. In these ways the peculiar urgency of these decisions can be acknowledged without threatening the normative heart of the doctrine of informed consent—that the free and informed refusal of a decisionally capable patient must be respected.

Our second question concerned what is to count as life-sustaining medical treatment. The general, and obvious, answer is any form of treatment whose withholding or withdrawal would (probably or certainly) hasten death. There are many unproblematic instances, such as chemotherapy for cancer and renal dialysis for kidney failure. But other instances may seem less clear. Consider the case of a patient whose esophageal cancer precludes both oral ingestion of food and water and its delivery by way of a nasogastric tube. Nutrition and hydration may still be provided to the patient through a gastrostomy tube introduced through the abdominal wall. There is little doubt that administering food and water in this way can be life-sustaining. The question that has been the subject of some debate is whether it constitutes medical treatment or is instead just the same basic care that is provided to other patients when their meals are delivered on a tray.

Before proceeding any further it is important to note that the answer to this question is unimportant for decisionally capable patients since these patients have the same right to refuse nutrition and hydration as they do to refuse medical treatment. In terms of the exercise of this right, it is a matter of indifference whether the patient is capable of taking food and water orally or must have it delivered artificially; force-feeding the patient by mouth would be as gross an invasion of his or her body as would implanting a tube against his or her will. Refusal of nutrition and hydration is therefore an ethical (and legal) end-of-life option available to decisionally capable patients alongside refusal of treatment. Indeed, some writers have argued that the availability of this option makes legalization of any form of physician-assisted death unnecessary.[4]

The question of the status of artificial feeding has therefore been debated largely for the case of decisionally incapable patients, principally those suffering from advanced dementia or permanent unconsciousness. Some institutions, such as the Catholic Church, have taken the position that feeding tubes may not be removed from such patients since artificially delivered nutrition and hydration constitutes basic care rather than medical treatment, and the same view has had some defenders in the bioethical literature.[5] However, over the past couple of decades it has been decisively rejected by the courts and the major medical organizations in the United States,[6] and it now represents a minority view among bioethicists. This consensus notwithstanding, many clinicians and laypersons alike continue to think that there is something about withdrawing food and water from a patient that makes it significantly different from withdrawing chemotherapy or dialysis.

But what is the difference? It cannot consist in the fact that food and water are basic necessities of life since oxygen is an even more basic necessity but no one denies that attaching a patient to a ventilator is a form of medical treatment. Might it have to do with cause of death? The orthodox view is that when a patient dies following withdrawal of life-sustaining treatment the cause of death is the patient's disease condition. When food and water are withdrawn, however, death might be attributed instead to starvation (or, more properly, dehydration). This appears to be the thought that has led some to contend that withdrawal of nutrition and hydration is a form of euthanasia.[7]

However, it seems more likely that our discomfort about ceasing to feed a patient has something to do with the social meaning of food. Eating and drinking together are important social events for us, and providing food for another, especially a child, is an essential part of nurturing. (By contrast, we do not normally have to provide or administer oxygen; it's just there.) Ceasing to feed someone therefore runs against the grain for us in a way in which ceasing to administer chemotherapy or dialysis or even oxygen does not; most of us have no experience of providing these things for another in our daily life. It is not surprising, therefore, that the withdrawal of nutrition and hydration, however artificial its means of delivery might be, has a different feel for us. The fact remains, however, that the implantation of a gastrostomy (or nasogastric) tube is an invasive medical procedure—one furthermore that carries with it a known risk of complications.[8] If a decisionally capable patient refuses to have the tube implanted or requests that it be withdrawn once implanted, then he or she is refusing medical treatment, and this refusal has the same ethical and legal force as the refusal of any other form of bodily invasion.

What is pain management?

The final stage of life need not go badly. In the best cases people die peacefully, without significant discomfort, in familiar surroundings, and in the company of their loved ones. Unfortunately, however, the end of life does not always live up to this ideal. In the developed world most people no longer die at home but in institutions where they are surrounded by strangers and vulnerable to fear, anxiety, and depression. For many the dying process is accompanied by such distressing physical symptoms as pain, shortness of breath, nausea, dizziness, agitation, or delirium.

In pursuit of its mission to prevent and relieve suffering due to pain and other physical symptoms, palliative medicine has a wide variety of pharmacological resources at its disposal, of which the best-known and most discussed are analgesics and sedatives. Most cancer patients in the advanced stages of their disease will experience pain severe enough to require treatment by means of analgesics. The World Health Organization has proposed the use of an "analgesic ladder" in the treatment of cancer pain, beginning with a non-narcotic and progressing through weaker to stronger opioids. When patients request pain relief, the physician is meant to ascend this ladder to the point where the analgesic of choice is sufficient either to eliminate the pain entirely or, failing that, to reduce it to a level that the patient finds tolerable. The location of this point will vary from case to case, but there is no question that for many patients only high doses of the strongest opioids, such as morphine or its derivatives, will suffice. In such cases it is standard clinical practice to increase the dosage or the frequency of infusions as the severity of cancer pain increases. At every stage the aim is to provide the minimum dose sufficient to control the pain: enough but not more than enough.

The use of high doses of opioids is now a standard technique in palliative medicine for the alleviation of refractory and intolerable symptoms during the dying process. However, it has been the subject of some controversy on the ground that in the process of relieving suffering it may also hasten death. Morphine in high doses has known side effects, the most serious of which is respiratory depression. Since depressed respiration can itself be a cause of death, there has been much concern that escalating doses of morphine might have the effect of shortening the patient's life, even if at each stage the dose is no more than the necessary minimum to control pain.

Even if this should turn out to be true, it would not follow that the administration of opioids to patients is either unethical or unlawful as long as the intent of the treatment is to relieve suffering rather than to hasten death. The ethical issues, including the significance of intention, will be explored later (in Chapter 4). Meanwhile, we should note that it is doubtful that opioids, even in high doses, do actually have the effect of hastening death. After an extensive review of the available evidence on opioid use, Susan Fohr draws the following conclusion:

> It is important to emphasize that there is no debate among specialists in palliative care and pain control on this issue. There is a broad consensus that when used appropriately, respiratory depression from opioid analgesics is a rarely occurring side effect. The belief that palliative care hastens death is counter to the experience of physicians with the most experience in this area. No studies have shown that patients' lives have been shortened through the administration of appropriate pain medication.[9]

On the contrary, Fohr argues, "the correct use of morphine is more likely to prolong a patient's life ... because he is more rested and pain-free." While the administration of opioids does carry a known risk of respiratory depression, the risk is highest when opioids are first begun. Thereafter, pain acts as a natural antagonist to this effect, and as the level of pain increases, so does tolerance to the effect. Increasing doses of morphine, therefore, need not raise the risk of causing death by depressing respiration.

If Fohr's conclusion is correct, then the "appropriate" use of opioids is seldom, if ever, a cause of death. However, her principal concern is the widespread belief among physicians that large doses of opioids will hasten the deaths of their patients, despite the lack of clinical evidence for this effect. This belief may lead physicians to undertreat serious pain, leaving their patients to suffer unnecessarily.

However this might be, it is in any case no easy matter to determine cause of death in the kinds of end-of-life situations we are now envisaging. Doses of morphine large enough to risk side effects such as respiratory depression will normally be used to relieve only the most severe pain. Timothy Quill reports that "some dying patients experience a 'crescendo' of pain just prior to dying, requiring rapidly escalating doses of analgesics."[10] It seems likely, therefore, that many patients die shortly after having been administered these "rapidly escalating doses," but it does not, of course, follow that they died because of them. In many such cases the analgesic will not be a cause of death, while in others it will be simply impossible to determine cause of death with any degree of certainty.

What is terminal sedation?

Most cancer pain can be successfully controlled by means of analgesics—most, but not all. A minority of patients at some stage of the dying process will experience pain (or other refractory physical symptoms) that cannot be adequately managed by administration of even the most powerful narcotics. Quill estimates this minority to be somewhere in the 2%–5% range; for these patients "the dose of opioids and sedatives must sometimes be increased to the point where the patient loses conscious awareness of their suffering."[11]

As defined earlier, *palliative* or *terminal sedation* is the practice of maintaining a patient in a state of deep and continuous unconsciousness until the point of death. On the question of whether it has the effect of hastening death, terminal sedation has been even more controversial than the administration of opioids since there is a greater risk of respiratory depression when the patient is unconscious. Like opioid use, terminal sedation is widely believed by physicians to be a cause of death. However, there is a crucial distinction to keep in mind here. Terminal sedation is almost invariably accompanied by withholding or withdrawing artificial nutrition and hydration. Since lack of food and water is a recognized cause of death, it is important to disentangle this effect from the possible life-shortening impact of the sedation itself. But when we do so, there may not be much residual impact left. A number of studies have cast doubt on the likelihood that sedatives prescribed at levels appropriate for symptom control at the end of life, up to and including deep continuous sedation, will shorten patients' lives.[12]

What is physician-assisted death?

The end-of-life treatment options we have surveyed so far—refusal of life-sustaining treatment, aggressive pain management, and terminal sedation—are all relatively uncontroversial from an ethical standpoint (with the exception of some issues we have noted along the way). They are also legal in most jurisdictions, including the United States. However, our main topic is another end-of-life option that is neither ethically uncontroversial nor legal (except in a few places). So we need to be sure we understand exactly what physician-assisted death (PAD) is.

As we have seen, there are many ways in which physicians (and other health care providers) may assist their patients through the dying process. Furthermore, as we have also seen, at least some of these ways may have the effect of hastening the patient's death. However, PAD refers exclusively to one particular way in which a doctor may help to hasten a patient's death: by providing the patient with medication (typically a barbiturate) at a dose level that is intended to cause death and that does in fact cause death. There are two ways in which this may occur. In *physician-assisted suicide* the doctor prescribes the medication for the patient, who then self-administers it orally. In *physician-administered euthanasia* the doctor administers the medication to the patient intravenously or by means of an injection. The difference between these two forms of PAD is strictly one of agency: who ends up actually administering the medication to the patient. In either case the administration of the medication is the immediate, or proximate, cause of the patient's death.

As the phrase suggests, PAD (in either form) is something done by a physician: it is *physician*-assisted death. So, while it is possible for others (family, friends, etc.) to assist someone's death, even by providing or administering a lethal dose of medication, we are confining ourselves here to cases in which this is done by a doctor (or by another health care provider, such as a nurse, under the direction of a doctor).

Unlike patient refusal of life-sustaining treatment, PAD involves administering treatment rather than withholding or withdrawing it. To put it differently, it is something that patients must request, not something they must refuse. In terms of a common (though misleading) distinction, PAD is therefore necessarily "active" (since it requires the administration of a lethal medication) rather than "passive." The phrase "active euthanasia" is therefore redundant, and "passive euthanasia" is a contradiction.

The best way to bring out the further features of PAD is to compare it to the other end-of-life treatment measures considered earlier. There are two important similarities among all of these measures. First, they all have at least the potential to hasten the patient's death. This is obviously true for PAD, in which the administration of the medication is the cause of death. But it is also true for refusal of life-sustaining treatment (on the assumption that the treatment refused would have extended the patient's life for however short a period) and for terminal sedation (at least on the assumption that the patient refuses artificial feeding and hydration while sedated) and may potentially be true for pain management (though, as we saw earlier, this is a matter of some controversy).

The second similarity is that all of these treatment options can be either voluntary or nonvoluntary. A treatment option is voluntary when it is requested (or, in the case of discontinuation of treatment, refused) by a patient who is decisionally capable at the time at which the treatment is to be administered. In our earlier example of the imaginary cancer patient Rebecca, refusal of treatment, pain management, and terminal sedation were all voluntary. But they can be nonvoluntary as well: in the case of a currently decisionally incapable patient life-sustaining treatment can be refused, or higher doses of opioids or sedatives can be requested, by substitute decision makers. The same can be true for PAD in the case of a patient currently incapacitated by conditions such as severe dementia or irreversible unconsciousness.

Voluntary end-of-life measures that have the effect of hastening death are easier to defend than nonvoluntary ones since in these cases the factor of patient autonomy is fully in play: the patient himself or herself is making an informed request (or refusal) at the time at which treatment will be initiated (or discontinued). The situation becomes much more complicated when the patient is not currently capable of making such a request and even more complicated for patients who have never had this capacity. To keep matters comparatively simple for as long as possible, we will confine attention in the next few chapters to voluntary PAD. We will take on the added complexities of nonvoluntary cases later (in Chapter 9).

There are equally important differences between PAD and the other end-of-life measures. One of these has to do with cause of death. In the case of PAD it is clear that the administration of the lethal medication is the immediate, or proximate, cause of death. This might also be said to be true for pain management or terminal sedation, if they do sometimes have the effect of shortening life. But in the case of treatment refusal it is at least arguable that the cause of death is the patient's illness (though this is less arguable when the treatment refused is artificial ventilation or nutrition and hydration). The other difference is a matter of intention. When a patient refuses further treatment, it may often be misleading, or just downright wrong, to say that he or she is thereby intending to hasten death (though the same exceptions might apply). We have also seen that high doses of opioids or sedatives are normally administered in order to minimize or eliminate patient suffering; if they ever also hasten the patient's death, then this is regarded as a further unintended effect. However, in the case of PAD the intent of the administration of the medication is precisely to cause death—or, to put it another way, to end the patient's suffering by bringing about death.

So PAD appears to differ from other end-of-life treatment options in terms of both causation and intention. It is these differences that are often thought to define an ethical "bright line" dividing PAD from these other, less controversial measures. Whether they actually do so we will determine later (in Chapter 4).

3

WHAT IS THE ETHICAL CASE IN FAVOR OF PHYSICIAN-ASSISTED DEATH?

What is the argument from well-being?

We now begin our inquiry into the ethical status of physician-assisted death, stating the case in favor in this chapter and the case against in the next. The former task is relatively straightforward since the principal arguments for the ethical justifiability of PAD invoke the same two basic values we have already encountered in our discussion of end-of-life measures: patient well-being and patient autonomy.

The first argument is based on a very simple and intuitively compelling proposition: suffering is intrinsically bad and therefore something to be prevented or relieved when possible. As we have seen, the relief of suffering during the dying process is one of the principal aims of palliative medicine. Most end-of-life suffering can be effectively controlled by adequate management of adverse physical symptoms, especially pain. However, not all suffering is physical, and not all physical suffering can be relieved by these means. It is in some of these refractory cases that terminal sedation becomes an option. At least part of the justification for the use of terminal sedation lies in its capacity to spare the patient needless additional suffering during the dying process. But this justification obviously applies equally to PAD. Patient well-being therefore provides a strong ethical case in favor of this option.

Before looking more closely at this argument, it would be useful to clarify somewhat the concept of suffering. Clearly, one of the main issues for dying patients is pain, and much of palliative medicine quite understandably focuses on providing adequate pain control. However, besides the fact that not all pain can be effectively controlled, it is important to understand that not all suffering is due to pain. The concepts of pain and suffering, though related, are quite distinct. Pain is best understood as a certain distinctive feeling or sensation to which we are normally (though not necessarily) averse. Pain normally causes us to suffer, but so do many other physical sensations that we find disagreeable: nausea, dizziness, itching, fatigue, shortness of breath, and so on. None of these is quite the same as pain, but each can be a component of suffering. Furthermore, while most—perhaps all—pain has an organic basis, many of the most familiar forms of suffering are psychological: anxiety, depression, despair, hopelessness, abandonment, rejection, humiliation, indignity, and so on. Suffering is therefore best understood broadly as encompassing any experience or condition of life to which we are strongly averse. It is the aversiveness of suffering—the fact that we hate it and want to be rid of it—that makes suffering bad for us. And it is the fact that suffering is bad for the one who experiences it that makes it intrinsically bad and thereby gives us all an ethical reason for wanting to prevent or relieve it.

No one seriously disputes that suffering is intrinsically bad and therefore something to be prevented or relieved, if possible. The whole enterprise of palliative care is organized around the assumption that patient suffering calls for a response and, when possible, intervention for the purpose of amelioration. Affirming the intrinsic badness of suffering need not lead us to deny that it can sometimes be extrinsically good. We can learn by suffering, not least about our own resources for coping with it. On the other hand, extravagant claims are sometimes made to the effect that suffering builds character or that we need to suffer in order to appreciate the good things in life. There may be some measure of truth to these claims, but it would be cruel to bring them into play for patients who are suffering through the dying process. For them there will be no future goods to compensate for the present evil. Because their suffering will be of no extrinsic value to them, and thus entirely pointless, they are left with just the intrinsic badness of it.

The argument from well-being to the justifiability of PAD can take a number of different forms. On the one hand, it might be consequentialist, resting simply on the fact that, given their circumstances, assisted death would provide the best outcome for some patients since it would avoid a great evil for them. This would not, of course, be sufficient to show that it would have the best overall consequences since it might adversely affect the interests of others. If friends and family have no desire to see their loved ones suffer and if they agree that hastening death would be best in these circumstances, then it seems unlikely that any harms to others could be found that would outweigh the great harm to the patient of continued suffering. We can hold this remote possibility open by saying that, for the consequentialist, the avoidance of further suffering for dying patients provides a strong presumptive reason in favor of PAD. However, in nearly all circumstances, that reason is certain also to be conclusive.

But the argument need not be consequentialist. Deontological arguments focus not on what would produce the best overall outcome but on the kinds of duties we owe to one another. It is very common to think that one of these is the duty to relieve suffering. This duty might be role-specific, attaching to physicians (and other health care providers) as part of their more general duty of care for their patients. Or it might be quite general, applying to anyone who is in a position to prevent or relieve serious suffering. In either case, the duty need be no more than presumptive, to leave open the possibility that some ways of acting on it might be prohibited by other (role-specific or general) duties. In the absence of such countervailing considerations, it would be conclusive.

What is the argument from autonomy?

One ethically significant fact about PAD is that it can be in a patient's best interest by preventing further pointless suffering. But it is not the only such fact: it is equally significant that by requesting PAD patients at the end of life are attempting to manage the timing and manner of their death. They are thereby choosing to die sooner, by medically assisted means, rather than wait for their illness to dictate the time and manner of their departure. For them, therefore, a request for PAD is an exercise of their autonomy. The value of autonomy thus grounds the second important argument for the justifiability of PAD.

As outlined in the previous chapter, autonomy (or self-determination) is a matter of being the active manager of one's life in accordance with one's own deeply held goals and values. In that earlier discussion, autonomy (along with well-being) was one of the values served by informed consent to treatment (and therefore informed refusal of treatment). But being the active manager of one's dying process may require requests for treatment as well as refusals. We have seen this already with respect to the treatment modalities discussed in the previous chapter. If the suffering of a competent patient reaches intolerable levels and he or she makes an informed request for either high-dose opioids or terminal sedation, then respecting that request serves both the patient's well-being and his or her autonomy, even though it may also hasten death. The same holds for a request for PAD.

The argument from autonomy can also be either consequentialist or deontological. On the one hand, we can say that when acceding to a patient request for PAD serves both his or her best interest and his or her autonomy, then we have even more reason to think that it would be best on the whole. But for this argument the more common form is deontological, resting on a right to self-determination. As we saw earlier (Chapter 2), requiring informed consent to treatment and honoring informed refusal of treatment are usually justified by reference to such a right: how things are to go with his or her body and life is a matter for the patient to decide. But the right of self-determination is also engaged by requests for treatment, such as analgesics or terminal sedation. And again this will hold equally if the request is for PAD.

When is PAD justified?

The arguments from well-being and autonomy provide the basic justificatory framework for PAD. However, they do not, and cannot, show that this practice is always justified. On the contrary, appeals to these values are capable of justifying PAD only under appropriate conditions. One such set of conditions would be the following:

Request. Because we are dealing (so far) with voluntary PAD, it must be requested by the patient and not on the patient's behalf by a substitute decision maker.

Capacity. The patient must be decisionally capable at the time with respect to the treatment option in question.

Decisional capacity includes the ability to understand and appreciate the nature and consequences of requesting a therapeutic intervention that is intended to cause death and will cause death. While decisional capacity must be the default presumption for adult patients, it is rebuttable by evidence of either some standing mental illness or disability or some situational factors serious enough to impair cognitive functioning. The relevant decisional capacity for assisted death is the ability to make reasoned decisions *with respect to this kind of treatment*. A person may be competent to make other personal decisions (such as financial ones) or even other treatment decisions but not this one.

Voluntariness. The patient's request must be free of undue influence and coercion, whether by providers or by family or friends. It is recognized, of course, that our decision-making as patients will often be influenced by what others think or suggest or by our knowledge of what they want or would prefer. Since it would aim much too high to purge decision-making of all such influences, the issue of voluntariness will turn on when such influences are "undue"— that is, when they rise to the level of fraud, deceit, duress, or any other form of coercion. As with decisional capacity, there will inevitably be borderline cases in which the voluntariness of a patient request for assisted death is uncertain.

Disclosure. The patient must be provided with adequate information concerning the treatment options in question. This information will normally include the patient's diagnosis and prognosis in the absence of treatment (including any uncertainty attending these matters), the nature of each of the available treatment options, the probable outcome of each option, and the risks attached to each option. The general rule for disclosure is that it should include all of the information that a reasonable person *in this particular patient's circumstances* would need in order to make a reasoned decision concerning the treatment in question.

Diagnosis. The patient must be diagnosed with a medical condition (an illness or disability) sufficiently serious to warrant consideration of treatment options that will hasten death. The condition need not itself be terminal. The patient must be experiencing a degree of suffering that he or she regards as intolerable and that cannot be alleviated by any other treatment option acceptable to the patient.

Of these five conditions, the first four simply replicate the standard conditions for informed consent to treatment that were enumerated in the previous chapter. The fifth, however, is specific to treatment decisions that will hasten death. It has, of course, been formulated here so as to apply to requests for PAD. However, it should also be applied to requests for high-dose opioids or terminal sedation (on the assumption that these methods of treatment also have the potential to hasten death). The reason for requiring that other treatment options have first been exhausted or that they have been refused by the patient is straightforward: hastening death is final and irreversible, precluding all further opportunity for rethinking one's choice. There is a mild degree of paternalism at work here—some privileging of patient well-being over autonomy—in ensuring that assisted death is not requested prematurely or unnecessarily.

Is there an ethical difference between the two forms of PAD?

The foregoing arguments apply equally to both forms of PAD: physician-assisted suicide and physician-administered euthanasia. However, we have not yet considered the possibility that there might be an ethical difference between the two. As we have defined them in the previous chapter, the distinction between them lies in the physician's role: providing lethal medication for the patient to self-administer versus administering it to the patient himself or herself.

Does this difference make an ethical difference? In principle it could. In the one case the patient causes his or her own death, while in the other his or her death is caused by a second party: the one is suicide, the other homicide (understood simply in its technical sense as the intentional killing of another person, with no implication that it is in any way wrongful). However, while this shift of agency does move us into a distinct ethical domain, it is difficult to see how the ethical status of the act could be different if all other factors remain constant. While homicide is normally wrongful—as in murder—it can also be justified—as in cases of self-defense. When homicide is wrongful it has two key features: it harms the victim (by depriving him or her of a valuable life) and it violates the victim's autonomy (by ending that life without the victim's consent). If a patient exercises his or her autonomy to make a rational, considered, stable request to hasten death and if that request is in his or her best interest, then neither of these wrong-making features of homicide would apply to the physician's act. If the physician would be justified in assisting the patient's suicide, it therefore follows that he or she would be equally justified in administering euthanasia.

4

WHAT IS THE ETHICAL
CASE AGAINST?

What is the right to life?

Making the case in favor of physician-assisted death was
a relatively straightforward exercise. Whether it took a
consequentialist or a deontological form, the argument appealed to the two basic values of patient well-being and
patient autonomy, the same values that support the other
forms of end-of-life treatment. Stating the case against PAD
is a more complicated matter since a number of different
arguments have been used to show that it is ethically unacceptable. All of these arguments are deontological in struc-
ture since they attempt to show that PAD violates either a
basic right or a basic duty. Opponents of PAD can therefore
concede that it might be in a patient's best interest and an
exercise of the patient's autonomy but contend that it is
nonetheless wrong. Their strategy consists in identifying
some feature that is claimed to be unique to PAD and that
defines an ethical "bright line" between PAD and these
other options. Different oppositional arguments rest on
different claims about what that feature is.

One of the defining features of PAD is that the administration of a lethal medication is the immediate or proximate
cause of the patient's death. If the medication is administered by a physician, then it seems that the physician has

killed the patient. But killing someone, it will be argued, violates that person's right to life and is therefore wrong. The concept of a right to life is a much-contested one, but whatever else it might be thought to entail it surely includes, at a minimum, the right not to be killed by another. Murder would, of course, violate that right, but, the argument goes, so would physician-administered euthanasia (PAE). The effect of this argument is to deny the ethical significance of one of the distinctions between PAE and murder. If you murder me, then you kill me against my will, whereas PAE involves ending my life with my consent or at my request. If my right to life imposes on you a duty not to kill me, then you violate that duty if you kill me, whether I have consented or not.

In the previous chapter we inquired whether there might be an ethical distinction between PAE and physician-assisted suicide (PAS). This construal of a right to life might support such a distinction if the duty not to kill is imposed only on others and not on oneself. On this view I would not violate my right to life by killing myself, nor would you violate it by assisting me in doing so, but you would violate it by killing me. However, the duty can also be understood as applying to any form of consensual killing, whether it be homicide or suicide. In that case it would equally prohibit both PAE and PAS. However, in order to assess the argument in its strongest form, we will continue here to focus on PAE.

This argument for the wrongness of PAE depends on a hidden premise: that the right to life is, in an important sense, inalienable. There are two different ways in which the right to life (interpreted as the right not to be killed) might be alienated: by *relinquishing* it or by *waiving* it. Each of these ways would involve canceling or annulling the duty that it imposes on others. If I relinquish the right, then I give it up irrevocably or abandon it so that no one in the future would have any duty not to kill me. Since that would leave my life bereft of all protection against others, there is good reason to deny that the right to life includes the power to relinquish it. On the other hand, if I waive the right, then I annul the duty imposed on a particular other person on a particular occasion. It is this power to waive the right not to have one's body touched or invaded by another, exercised by informed consent, that permits physicians to treat their patients. Consenting to, or requesting, PAE is another exercise of this power; since it cancels the physician's duty not to kill me, the physician does no wrong in providing that kind of treatment.

The argument from the right to life to the wrongness of PAE therefore requires that the right be inalienable in this second way—that it cannot be waived. But this step in the argument runs up against the fact that for some patients at the end of life, waiving the right would be both in their best interest and an exercise of their autonomy. Whereas there might be a convincing case to be made against the power to relinquish one's right to life, there seems no similar case against the power to waive it (under certain conditions). Indeed, it would seem perverse to insist that the inalienability of a patient's right to life prevents him or her from accessing an end-of-life treatment option that would be best for him or her and that he or she is autonomously choosing.

What is the sanctity of life?

There is another way to exploit the intuitively appealing idea that what makes PAD (in either of its forms) distinctive is the fact that the patient is killed (whether by himself or herself or by another). This argument turns on the claim that PAD thereby violates the sanctity of human life. The common idea behind sanctity-of-life principles is that human life is somehow "sacred"—that is, it has some kind of value or status weighty enough to rule out most cases of the intentional taking of life, whether one's own or that of another. There may be some cases in which intentional killing does not engage this value or in which it is outweighed by a competing value, but these cases will be rare and exceptional. They will not include PAD.

There are two forms of deontology that share this common idea but interpret it in radically different ways. We may call them Thomistic and Kantian since they are inspired by the theories of Thomas Aquinas and Immanuel Kant, respectively. According to both theories the wrong-making feature of PAD lies in its violation of a kind of respect that we owe to everyone, including ourselves. The theories part company, however, on the precise object or target of this respect. For the Thomists respect is owed to the fundamental goods that constitute a person's well-being or human fulfillment, whereas for the Kantians it is owed to the person himself or herself. The two deontological traditions converge in most (though possibly not all) of their practical implications, including the condemnation of PAD in both of its forms, but they reach this common ground from quite different starting points.

The Thomistic (or natural law) tradition begins with a conception of human well-being as consisting in a plurality of goods, such as knowledge, aesthetic experience, and friendship.[1] Each of these goods is independent of and irreducible to the others, and each makes an intrinsic, and not merely instrumental, contribution to human fulfillment or flourishing. Morality then enters the picture in the form of an injunction to respect each of these goods in every act, which is interpreted to mean that one must never "choose directly against a basic good" or "choose to destroy, damage, or impede some instance of a basic good for the sake of an ulterior end."[2] On this view respect for a person consists in respect for the fundamental goods that constitute that person's well-being. This respect is owed equally to the goods of all persons, including one's own. The theory therefore makes room for the idea of duties to oneself, consisting in duties not to "destroy, damage, or impede" any of one's own fundamental goods. The prohibition of both homicide and suicide is then entailed by the fact that life itself is one of those fundamental goods. Any intentional taking of life, whether one's own or that of another, will constitute the choice to destroy a fundamental good and is forbidden for that reason.

The case this theory builds against both forms of PAD obviously rests in part on the claim that life itself is a fundamental aspect of human well-being. So we are entitled to ask what is here meant by *life*. Earlier (in Chapter 1) we found two distinct concepts of life: biological and personal. Briefly, biological life consists in the integrated functioning of the organism and is possible after the irreversible cessation of all capacity for consciousness or experience, while personal life requires the capacity for whatever psychological states are constitutive of a person. For human beings the two normally go hand in hand, but they can diverge in pathological conditions such as permanent vegetative state, in which the person remains biologically alive but with no consciousness whatever. So is it biological or personal life that, in the Thomistic view, is a fundamental human good? In some contexts it seems to be a robust version of the latter. Thus John Finnis writes, "The term 'life' here signifies every aspect of the vitality (*vita*, life) which puts a human being in good shape for self-determination. Hence, life here includes bodily (including cerebral) health, and freedom from the pain that betokens organic malfunctioning or injury."[3] But it seems obvious that this cannot be the conception of life that will support an absolute (or near-absolute) prohibition of consensual killing.

Patients who are motivated to seek PAD do not enjoy a life in this sense, so their death would not destroy a fundamental good for them. More generally, in this conception of life it would be difficult, if not impossible, to condemn any instance of PAD undertaken to escape intolerable suffering brought about by a serious medical condition.

This unwelcome implication has been duly noted by the proponents of the Thomistic theory, who have come to defend the view that mere biological life, in the absence of all capacity for personal life, is still a basic human good.[4] Since every instance of PAD necessarily destroys biological life, every instance of PAD will qualify as choosing directly against a basic good. This contention—that biological life is in itself an intrinsic good for a person—plays an indispensable role in the Thomistic/natural law condemnation of PAD. Critics, however, have found the contention deeply implausible. Jonathan Glover, for instance, has written,

> I have no way of refuting someone who holds that being alive, even though unconscious, is intrinsically valuable. But it is a view that will seem unattractive to those of us who, in our own case, see a life of permanent coma as in no way preferable to death. From the subjective point of view there is nothing to choose between the two.... For permanently comatose existence is subjectively indistinguishable from death, and unlikely often to be thought intrinsically preferable to it by people thinking of their own future.[5]

The view that Glover finds much more plausible is that biological life matters not in its own right but because it is a necessary condition of everything that does matter: "If life is worth preserving only because it is the vehicle for consciousness, and consciousness is of value only because it is necessary for something else, then that 'something else' is the heart of this particular objection to killing. It is what is meant by a 'life worth living' or a 'worth-while life.'"[6] Proponents of the Thomistic theory have recognized that they must hold the line on this point; if life has value only as a condition of whatever else is valuable for a person, then the case against PAD undertaken to end serious suffering will collapse. However, both Glover's negative point (against the intrinsic value of merely biological life) and his positive proposal enjoy a great deal of support from common sense. It is difficult for most people to discern any value in the life of a permanently comatose patient *for that patient*—any contribution that his or her life is making to his or her well-being.

Suppose, however, that the claim is true. Suppose, that is, that bare biological life is intrinsically valuable regardless of any other goods it might contain or make possible. The impermissibility of PAD will not follow from this claim alone. For it might be that the value of bare life is comparatively slight compared to the value of the other goods, so that a life that lacked all of these other goods would itself be of only slight value. Furthermore, if that life contained serious suffering, then the disvalue of the suffering might exceed the value of being alive so that on balance the person's (continued) life would not be worth living. Since this is arguably the condition of many patients at the end of life, PAD might be justifiable after all as being in their overall best interest.

The Thomistic theory blocks this conclusion by virtue of its principle that one must never "choose to destroy, damage, or impede some instance of a basic good for the sake of an ulterior end." If a patient were to request PAD, then he or she would be choosing to destroy one basic good (life) for the sake of another (freedom from suffering). So now we need to ask why, in the Thomistic view, it is always wrong to intentionally "destroy, damage, or impede" one fundamental good for the sake of pursuing another. Friendship and knowledge are two such goods, but it seems that, for the sake of his or her overall own well-being, a person might rationally choose to damage or impede the former for the sake of the latter—for instance, by cutting ties with some friends in order to make time for important research. Any deontological principle that rules out these trade-offs would appear to be unreasonably rigoristic. But if trade-offs are permissible, then why would it necessarily be wrong to give up the slight value of life in order to achieve the much greater value of putting an end to suffering?

The problems that the Thomistic theory encounters seem to stem from the fact that it starts with a list of fundamental human goods and then interprets respect for persons as respect for these goods. If a more plausible sanctity-of-life argument against PAD is to be found, then it must start with a different conception of respect. Alan Donagan, who is acutely aware of the Thomistic tradition, has contrasted its idea of respecting basic human goods with the Kantian idea of respecting human nature as an end in itself and has argued for the superiority of the latter. Donagan defends the fundamental principle that "it is impermissible not to respect every human being, oneself or any other, as a rational creature."[7] This principle then supports a duty not to injure or hurt persons, whether oneself or others. Since the worst injury anyone can inflict on another (or on himself or herself) is death, it follows in Donagan's version of Kantian theory that PAD is impermissible.

Actually, this conclusion follows only if PAD inflicts a harm or injury on the patient. It does, of course, intentionally cause the patient's death, but we have already found reason to think that death can sometimes be a benefit, rather than a harm, for a patient at the end of life (and would be so for many patients motivated to seek PAD). Donagan's

Kantian case for the wrongness of PAD is therefore seriously incomplete. It is incomplete in another way as well since Donagan never makes it very clear why consenting to one's own death (whether through PAS or PAE) would constitute failure to respect oneself as a rational creature. If a patient opts for either form of PAD in order to escape further suffering, there seems no reason to think that he or she is thereby disrespecting himself or herself as a person or a rational being. Insofar as his or her rationality is at issue at all, the considered decision to hasten death can be seen as an expression of that rational nature rather than a perversion of it. A free and informed request for PAD, in either of its forms, would seem to be an exercise of autonomy or self-determination in a way that does no harm to any other persons. For anyone who values autonomy there should be much to like in such a decision.

It seems difficult, therefore, to make a convincing case against PAD on sanctity-of-life grounds. We have not, of course, canvassed all imaginable ways of interpreting this idea, and thus we cannot rule out the possibility that such a case can be made. But the two interpretations of the sanctity of life that we have considered—Thomistic and Kantian—have been by far the most prominent and influential among deontologists who have invoked this kind of principle. If neither of them is capable of withstanding critical scrutiny, then we still lack a conclusive ethical case against PAD.

What is the doctrine of double effect?

We have so far been working with the idea that PAD is morally objectionable because it constitutes killing, thereby violating either the right to life or the sanctity of life. While this has not yet produced a convincing case against PAD, we might do better with a somewhat more fine-grained analysis. PAD, it could be argued, differs from all of the other end-of-life treatment options in two important respects: it is intended to cause the patient's death and it is in fact the cause of death. PAD is therefore unique in terms of both intention and causation. The argument then proceeds by claiming that at least one of these distinctive features enables us to define the ethical "bright line" that separates PAD from the other end-of-life treatment modalities. So we now need to assess these arguments from intention and causation. We begin with intention in this section and turn to causation in the next.

It is certainly true that the patient's death is the intended outcome of PAD, in either of its forms. Patients seek PAD as a means of avoiding or preventing further suffering at the end of life. As such, the patient's death is a means to the end of preventing suffering, and if the end is intended, then so is the means to it. In this, PAD can be contrasted with two other end-of-life treatment measures: the administration of high-dose opioids for pain control and terminal sedation. In both of these cases the intended aim of the treatment is relief of suffering. Should the patient's death also thereby be hastened, then that would be an unintended, though possibly foreseen, side effect of the treatment. It is this distinction between death as the intended effect of treatment and death as an unintended but foreseen effect that marks the difference between PAD and these other ways of relieving suffering.

This intended/foreseen distinction will also differentiate PAD from many cases of refusal of treatment: those in which the patient's aim is not to hasten death but rather to avoid the severely distressing side effects of treatment that is likely to be futile in any case. This would be a plausible construal of the refusal by many end-stage cancer patients of further chemotherapy. They are not thereby seeking to die, just not to suffer from treatment that is unlikely to be effective at extending their lives. But it would fail for other cases in which the hastening of death seems clearly to be the patient's aim, as in the request for removal of a ventilator or feeding tube. These cases would then fall on the same side of the ethical "bright line" as PAD. The appeal to intention therefore will not quite suffice to isolate PAD as uniquely ethically objectionable.

However, we still need to ask whether intention marks a clear ethical distinction between acceptable and unacceptable end-of-life options. This focus on intention has been the most common and influential means of attempting to draw that "bright line" between PAD and all of the other end-of-life treatment options. The ethical significance of the intending/foreseeing distinction derives from the *doctrine of double effect*, which in its simplest form holds that it is impermissible to bring about a harm to a person as an intended effect, while it would be permissible (in otherwise identical conditions) to bring about the same harm as an unintended (and foreseeable) side effect. The origins of the doctrine are usually traced back to the thirteenth century in Thomas Aquinas's justification of killing in self-defense. By the sixteenth century it had become an established feature of Catholic moral thinking, but more recently it has broadened out to secular philosophy as well in its application to a wide range of moral problems including abortion and the killing of noncombatants in wartime. The doctrine undeniably yields intuitively plausible results in some ethical contexts. Many people, for instance, think that there is an important ethical difference between deliberately targeting innocent civilians in warfare and targeting military facilities even though doing so will foreseeably result in civilian casualties.

The argument against PAD that we are considering applies the doctrine to end-of-life cases in which the harm in question is death. But there it runs into a significant obstacle: as we have already seen (Chapter 1), for many dying patients who are experiencing great suffering death will be a benefit rather than a harm. The doctrine of double effect applies only to harms, not to benefits; it would be crazy to claim that it is wrong to confer a benefit on a person intentionally but not wrong to do so as an unintended side effect. In fact, when benefits are in question the reverse would seem to be true: better that they be intended (thus demonstrating good will) rather than unintended. In cases in which death would be a benefit rather than a harm, therefore, the doctrine of double effect just seems inapplicable. Since this is arguably the case whenever PAD would be indicated, the doctrine provides no reason to think that it is ethically impermissible.

What is the doctrine of doing and allowing?

If intention does not enable us to draw the requisite ethical "bright line," perhaps causation will fare better. It is certainly true that in PAD death is caused by the lethal dose of medication (whether self-administered by the patient or administered by the physician). In this PAD can be contrasted with at least most cases of refusal of treatment, in which, so the argument goes, the patient dies as a result of the underlying medical condition. In the former case the patient is killed; in the latter he or she is allowed to die. This killing/letting die distinction is often used to distinguish "active" from "passive" means of bringing about death, where PAD is "active," while cessation of treatment is merely "passive."

The killing/letting die distinction would not, however, differentiate PAD from aggressive pain management and terminal sedation. If there are instances in which these latter treatment measures hasten death, then they are helping to make it happen and not merely allowing it to happen. Indeed, it is far from clear that death is merely allowed to happen in every case of treatment cessation. Determining cause of death in these cases can be a very complicated and controversial matter. There are relatively clear cases, such as the refusal of further chemotherapy, in which it seems right to say that the patient dies of his or her cancer (though even here it is true that, but for the refusal of treatment, the patient would not have died then). But in other cases, such as refusal of a ventilator or of food and water, the withdrawal of treatment may be the (or at least a) cause of death since the patient may die not of the illness but of dehydration or lack of oxygen. These cases would then fall on the same side of the ethical "bright line" as PAD. Like intention, therefore, the appeal to causation will not quite suffice to isolate PAD as uniquely ethically objectionable.

In any case, the ethical significance of the killing/letting die distinction derives from the broader principle that it is impermissible to inflict a harm on a person, while it would be permissible (in otherwise identical conditions) to allow the same harm to happen to him or her. This principle is commonly known as the *doctrine of doing and allowing*. Like the doctrine of double effect, the broader principle is intuitively appealing in some ethical contexts. Many people believe, for instance, that while it would clearly be wrong to kill a child, it is not wrong (or at least not as wrong) to fail to donate money to famine relief in Somalia, even though the donation would have prevented the death of a child. In the former case the child's death is made to happen by your action, while in the latter it is allowed to happen as a result of the famine.

However, even if the broader principle is intuitively appealing in some contexts, it does not apply to the end-of-life context with which we are working here. Like the doctrine of double effect, the doctrine of doing and allowing applies only to harms, not to benefits; it would be crazy to claim that it is wrong to confer a benefit on a person but not wrong to allow the same benefit to happen. (Again, the reverse seems more plausible.) The doctrine is therefore inapplicable to end-of-life scenarios in which death is a benefit for a patient and so can provide no support for the ethical "bright line" distinguishing PAD from the other forms of treatment.

Is there an ethical difference between PAD and other end-of-life treatment options?

Many people believe that there is an ethical "bright line" between PAD and the other means of alleviating suffering during the dying process. This thought gets articulated in various ways. Sometimes it is just that we are crossing some kind of important boundary when we allow doctors to kill their patients or to assist patients to kill themselves. At other times you hear slogans such as that doctors should "cure not kill" (ignoring the fact that the function of palliative care is not to cure but to manage patient symptoms).

However, it turns out to be surprisingly difficult to show that any such "bright line" exists. There are two reasons for this. The first is that the best justification for the other forms of end-of-life care—a justification that invokes the values of patient well-being and autonomy—seems to apply equally to PAD. The second is that there seems to be no difference between PAD and these other measures that makes an ethical difference. We have sought such a difference by appealing to notions like the right to life, the sanctity of life, intention, and causation. Undoubtedly, we have not examined all of the possibilities, so there still could be a way of securing that "bright line." But until we find it, we will have to conclude that if the three other treatment options can be ethically justified for dying patients, then so can PAD.

What role can be played in this issue by religious arguments?

Attentive readers will have noticed one significant omission in the succession of arguments we have considered both for and against the ethical justifiability of PAD: none of them have been religious. The question we are debating is one that many people answer by reference to their religious convictions and one on which most religious institutions have settled positions. Despite this, all of the arguments we have canvassed, on both sides of the question, have been thoroughly secular. The reason for this exclusion of religious arguments is most evident when we are trying to determine what the law governing PAD should be. In a religiously pluralistic society, public policy governing the conduct of all cannot be justified by reference to faith-based premises shared only by some: to violate this constraint is to violate freedom of conscience. And not just freedom of religious conscience. To be sure, imposing the religious beliefs of some on those of different faith denominations will violate the latters' freedom of religion. But the wrong is no less when the religious beliefs of some are imposed on those who have no such beliefs at all. Public debate about public policy must therefore be resolutely secular—that is, it must prescind from any views that can be defended only on religious grounds. That does not imply that the debate must be atheistic. To say that the debate prescinds from religious beliefs is to say that it takes no stand either way on the truth of such beliefs. Presupposing the truth of atheism would be as offensive to conscience as presupposing the truth of any set of theistic beliefs.

It may be less obvious why the inquiry into the ethics of PAD must also be secular, but the reason is ultimately the same. The ethical arguments to be considered in this book are aimed at all readers of good will regardless of their religious convictions (or, indeed, whether they have any). To base these arguments on any particular set of such convictions would be to limit the audience by excluding everyone who does not share them. There is a legitimate place for treatments of these issues that are aimed exclusively at a particular faith community, but this book is not one of them. Put another way, the arguments of this book are intended to appeal exclusively to the feature that unites people rather than divides them—their common rationality. As such, they presuppose that complex and challenging ethical issues, on which people of good will take starkly opposing positions, are nonetheless capable of rational resolution. Many readers will, of course, continue to base their ethical beliefs on a sacred text, the shared creed of a faith community, or their own personal convictions of what their god demands of them. Nothing in this book should be interpreted as suggesting that they should not do so. But to the extent that their ethical views are theistically based in this way they are also beyond rational challenge and debate.

5

WHAT IS THE HISTORY
OF LEGAL
PHYSICIAN-ASSISTED DEATH?

Is it legal for patients to refuse life-sustaining treatment?

Earlier (Chapter 2) we encountered the doctrine of informed consent as a cornerstone of biomedical ethics and noted how it entails the patient's right to refuse treatment. In addition to its ethical status, however, the doctrine has legal force. The requirement of informed consent to treatment was explicitly affirmed by the New York Court of Appeals in its 1914 *Schloendorff* decision.[1] The case involved a woman, Mary Schloendorff, who was admitted to New York Hospital complaining of a stomach disorder. During her stay there a fibroid tumor was diagnosed, for which surgery was recommended. Schloendorff refused consent for the surgery but did agree to an examination of the tumor under anesthesia. During this procedure the doctors went ahead with removal of the tumor. Schloendorff subsequently sued the hospital. In his judgment for the court Justice Cardozo stated the common law doctrine in the following terms: "Every human being of adult years and sound mind has a right to determine what shall be done with his own body; and a surgeon who performs an operation without his patient's consent commits an assault, for which he is liable in damages."

Decades later the doctrine was given its definitive statement in the 1947 Nuremberg Code, formulated in response to the medical experiments carried out both in prewar Nazi Germany and during the war in the concentration camps. The first clause of the code stated:

> The voluntary consent of the human subject is absolutely essential. This means that the person involved should have legal capacity to give consent; should be so situated as to be able to exercise free power of choice, without the intervention of any element of force, fraud, deceit, duress, overreaching, or other ulterior form of constraint or coercion; and should have sufficient knowledge and comprehension of the elements of the subject matter involved as to enable him to make an understanding and enlightened decision.[2]

Although the code was devised specifically to govern the use of human subjects in biomedical research, its basic principles were soon adapted to the clinical setting as well. Subsequent refinements of those principles have been shaped primarily by the courts as they have adjudicated actions brought by patients against health care providers and hospitals.

One of those refinements has involved explicit recognition that the consent requirement confers upon competent adults the right to refuse treatment, even when doing so is certain to hasten death. This right was affirmed for the refusal of nutrition and hydration in the 1986 *Bouvia* case.[3] Elizabeth Bouvia was a twenty-eight-year-old woman who was quadriplegic as a result of severe cerebral palsy. Except for a few fingers of one hand and some slight head and facial movements she was completely immobile and confined to a bed in a hospital. She was also in continual pain from degenerative and severely crippling arthritis, not all of which was being relieved by periodic doses of morphine. Despite her physical disabilities, she was intelligent and fully mentally competent. She was capable of being spoon-fed, but the hospital medical staff determined that she could not—or would not—take in enough nutrition by this means to keep her weight from falling to dangerously low levels. They therefore inserted a nasogastric feeding tube against her will and contrary to her express written instructions. Her petition for removal of the tube was denied by the trial court but then upheld by the California Court of Appeal, which affirmed her right to refuse this life-sustaining treatment.

The appellate court simply asserted, without argument, that the provision of food and water by means of a nasogastric tube constituted medical treatment. However, it did devote some attention to the question of whether in refusing the tube-feeding Ms. Bouvia was seeking to commit suicide. Despite evidence that she had earlier expressed a wish to die and had indeed attempted to starve herself to death, the court held that in petitioning for removal of the tube she was not intending to die but rather accepting an earlier death as a foreseeable outcome of her decision. In removing the tube, therefore, her physicians would not be assisting her suicide.

Similar issues arose a few years later in the 1992 Canadian case of *Nancy B.*[4] The plaintiff in that case was a twenty-five-year-old woman suffering from Guillain-Barré syndrome, an irreversible neurological disorder that had left her incapable of movement and dependent on a ventilator. Her intellectual capacity was unaffected by the disease. After two and a half years in this condition, she requested removal of the respiratory support in order to escape the suffering caused by her immobility. With the ventilator, she could potentially have lived for a long time;

without it, she would die quickly. While her decision was not opposed either by her health care providers or by the hospital, it was unclear whether under Canadian law disconnecting her from the ventilator would constitute criminal negligence causing death (a culpable homicide).

Justice Dufour, who heard the case in the Quebec Superior Court, affirmed Nancy B.'s legal right to refuse continued use of the ventilator, even though such refusal would precipitate her death. In determining whether placing a patient on a ventilator is a form of medical treatment, he reasoned as follows: "Of course it is a technique of the same nature as feeding a patient. One cannot therefore make a distinction between artificial feeding and other essential life-sustaining techniques." The cause of death, Dufour argued, would be the disease, not the removal of the ventilator. He therefore concluded that Nancy B. could not be considered to be committing suicide by refusing artificial respiration, even though she would certainly die without it, and that her physicians could not be liable for assisting a suicide. Five weeks after the judgment her attending physician induced Nancy B. into a coma and removed the ventilator; she died comfortably in her sleep.

By 1997, when the US Supreme Court upheld the constitutionality of New York's ban on physician-assisted suicide in its *Quill* decision, Chief Justice Rehnquist could acknowledge the patient's right of refusal in the opening sentence of his opinion: "In New York, as in most States, it is a crime to aid another to commit or attempt suicide, but patients may refuse even lifesaving medical treatment."[5] The right of a patient to refuse life-sustaining treatment—even treatment as basic as the administration of oxygen or of food and water—is therefore now settled doctrine in American law.

This is not, however, the end of the story. Despite their serious physical disabilities, both Elizabeth Bouvia and

Nancy B. were fully decisionally capable. The resolution of their cases therefore did not address the further issue of whether such treatment can be refused by substitute decision makers for patients who are not decisionally capable. This part of the story will be pursued later (in Chapter 9).

Is it legal to administer pain medication that may hasten death?

It is obvious that withholding or withdrawing life-sustaining treatment will in most cases result in hastening death, though the cause of death will normally be recorded as the underlying disease condition rather than the (non) treatment decision. But there are other ways in which physicians may legally hasten death, including the administration of narcotics, such as morphine, in order to control pain. As we saw earlier (Chapter 2), it is at least widely believed that if the pain is severe enough, then the dosage of medication necessary to bring it down to acceptable levels may also be sufficient to cause death. In such cases it can (and will) be argued that death is not the intended effect of the treatment; rather, the intended effect is pain relief, and hastening death is merely foreseen as a possible, or probable, side effect. As Rehnquist acknowledged in *Quill*, "The law has long used actors' intent or purpose to distinguish between two acts that may have the same result." He then applied this distinction specifically to the use of pain medication: "The same is true when a doctor provides aggressive palliative care; in some cases, painkilling drugs may hasten a patient's death, but the physician's purpose and intent is, or may be, only to ease his patient's pain."

In this way the courts have distinguished PAS from other end-of-life measures that may also have the effect of hastening the patient's death but are not intended to do so. However, they have also acknowledged, as Rehnquist put it, that "the line between the two may not be clear." In the event that a case comes to legal attention, physicians can avoid liability for hastening a patient's death by establishing (a) that the medication in question had a legitimate therapeutic function, such as pain relief; (b) that no more of it was administered than was necessary in order to achieve this result; and (c) that no other means was available of producing the same result without also hastening death.

Is terminal sedation legal?

As noted earlier (Chapter 2), terminal sedation is often also assumed to have the effect of hastening death. However this might be, patients who request it will usually also execute an advance directive refusing all other treatment, including nutrition and hydration, while sedated. The combined effect of this request for sedation and refusal of nutrition and hydration would then be to shorten life. Since each of these components can be perfectly lawful, as long as the usual conditions for informed consent and refusal are satisfied, their conjunction is presumptively lawful as well. Terminal sedation is therefore a standard, if extreme, measure available to patients and physicians in palliative care settings without risk of legal liability.

Where did any form of physician-assisted death first become legal?

In 1942 Switzerland adopted legislation that made it a crime to assist a suicide but with a significant loophole. Under article 115 of the Swiss Penal Code, "any person who, yielding to selfish motives, incites or assists an individual to commit suicide shall, in the case where suicide is achieved or attempted, be punished by up to five years' confinement or imprisonment."[6] The requirement of a selfish motive here was crucial since it logically implied that in the absence of such a motive, assisting a suicide would not be an offense.

So when is a motive for assisting a suicide selfish? According to the Swiss National Advisory Commission for Biomedical Ethics, a motive is "deemed to be selfish if the offender is *pursuing personal advantage*. Such gains may be of a material nature ... but also non-material or emotional (e.g., gratification of hatred, a desire for revenge, or spite)."[7] The further condition that must be satisfied in an assisted suicide concerns the mental capacity of the "victim." Article 16 of the Swiss Civil Code states that "mental capacity is possessed by anyone who does not lack the ability to act rationally on account of minority or as a result of mental illness, mental deficiency, inebriation, or similar conditions."[8] Assisting the suicide of a person deemed to lack mental capacity may be punishable as a homicide.

Nothing in article 115 requires that the person assisting a suicide be a physician, and the most distinctive feature of the Swiss situation is the role played by the various not-for-profit right-to-die organizations active in the country. The largest of these groups is Exit Deutsche Schweiz, currently numbering about 50,000 members. Since 1990 it has been providing active assistance with suicides for members who are "experiencing unbearable suffering or are disabled in a serious manner."[9] Members who wish an assisted suicide must approach Exit of their own free will, and the organization will provide the service only in those cases in which its criteria are met. Those criteria require that the applicant be adult, competent, and suffering from "a fatal illness, a severe disability deemed unacceptable, or unbearable pain for which there is no prospect of relief."[10] In order to avoid any suspicion of material gain from the suicide, Exit charges only a nominal annual membership fee and then offers all of its services to members at no additional charge. All applicants must be examined by a doctor, who, if satisfied that the criteria have been met, provides a prescription for a lethal dose of a barbiturate. Most Exit-assisted suicides take place in the patient's home, although a small number occur in nursing homes or in a room provided by the organization. Since 2006 some Swiss hospitals have allowed Exit-assisted suicides to be carried out on their premises, although no hospital staff are allowed to participate. After each death, the Exit volunteer who has attended it notifies the police, who, along with the medical examiner, conduct an investigation. If they are satisfied that there has been no violation of article 115, then no charges are laid. There is no central notification system in Switzerland to which cases of assisted suicide must be reported.

Essentially the same procedures are followed by Dignitas, which has facilitated well over 1,000 assisted suicides since 1998. The major difference between the two organizations is that Dignitas offers its services to nonresidents; its membership base of about 6,000 is drawn from fifty-two different countries around the world. The majority of persons who undergo Dignitas-assisted suicides are foreigners, with the largest numbers coming from Germany and Britain. Switzerland is the only country in the world to allow this "suicide tourism," a practice that has led to considerable domestic criticism of Dignitas's activities. Initiatives to change the law so as to prohibit this traffic have been suggested, but so far none has succeeded.

Because of the role played by the private right-to-die organizations, assisted suicide in Switzerland is much less closely regulated than it is in the other jurisdictions in which it is now legal. Nonetheless, "duty-of-care criteria" for these cases have been developed by both the Swiss Academy of Medical Sciences and the National Advisory Commission for Biomedical Ethics. Touching as they do on such familiar themes as patient decisional capacity, a voluntary and enduring request, the presence of "severe illness-related suffering," and an independent second opinion, these criteria are very similar to those that have been written into law in other countries. Although they have no legal force in Switzerland, they do serve the purpose of guiding police and medical examiners in deciding whether to pursue a prosecution for a suicide assisted by one of the organizations.

The issue of patient decisional capacity was tested in the Swiss Federal Tribunal in a case decided in November 2006. The complainant, known only as X. Y., was a fifty-three-year-old man with a severe bipolar affective disorder who had requested assistance with suicide from Dignitas. The organization was prepared to provide its usual services, but the physician consulted refused to provide a prescription for sodium pentobarbital. X. Y. then petitioned the court that Dignitas be allowed access to the medication without a prescription. When this request was refused in the lower courts, he appealed to the Federal Tribunal. The tribunal upheld the lower courts' decision that sodium pentobarbital should be dispensed only by prescription but also addressed the question of whether a person suffering from a severe mental illness could qualify for an assisted suicide:

> It cannot be denied that an incurable, long-lasting, severe mental impairment similar to a somatic one can create suffering out of which a patient would find his/her life in the long run not worth living anymore.... However, utmost restraint needs to be exercised. It is imperative to distinguish between a desire to die that is an expression of a treatable mental disorder requiring treatment and one that is based on a self-determined, carefully considered, and lasting

decision of a lucid person ("balance suicide") that may need to be respected.[11]

In this way the tribunal established that suffering due to a psychiatric disorder could be an acceptable ground for assisted suicide in Switzerland.

In light of subsequent developments in other jurisdictions, the Swiss model of legal physician-assisted death is atypical in certain respects. For one thing, the Swiss have legalized only PAS and not physician-administered euthanasia. The latter remains a criminal offense in Switzerland to this day, though with a reduced penalty. The Swiss are not the only jurisdiction to legalize PAS only; as we will see shortly, this is now the standard model in a number of American states. But Switzerland is the only European jurisdiction to maintain this restriction. Elsewhere in Europe where PAD is legal both forms are permitted.

Because of the role of not-for-profit agencies in facilitating PAS, it may also be technically incorrect to say that the Swiss have legalized *physician-assisted* suicide. However, as explained earlier, doctors are still the effective gatekeepers in the procedures followed by these agencies since they retain a monopoly on prescribing the drugs that clients will self-administer. As such, they have to be satisfied that each request conforms to the agency's stated criteria. In this, the Swiss model is not completely dissimilar to the situation in those American states that have legalized PAS, except that in these latter cases the criteria of eligibility are stated in law.

Where has PAE become legal?

The Netherlands was the first jurisdiction in the world to legalize both forms of PAD. The process by which this occurred was uniquely Dutch, extending as it did over a period of some thirty years before the law was formally amended to permit both PAS and PAE (under stipulated conditions). Both killing another at that person's own request and assisting the suicide of another had been expressly forbidden in articles 293 and 294 of the Dutch Criminal Code adopted in 1886. However, the former statute was put in question in 1973 by the case of Dr. Geertruida Postma, who administered a lethal dose of morphine to her seventy-eight-year-old mother, who was deaf, partially paralyzed, and confined to a wheelchair and who had pleaded with her daughter to end her suffering by ending her life. Dr. Postma alerted the authorities of her action and was prosecuted under article 293. At her trial she invoked the defense of necessity, arguing that she was faced with a conflict between her duty to preserve her mother's life and her duty to relieve her suffering. Article 40 of the Dutch Criminal Code explicitly allows for this defense: "Any person who commits an offence under the compulsion of an irresistible force shall not be criminally liable."[12] Because the morphine she had administered was an analgesic that could legitimately have been used to relieve suffering in her mother's circumstances, she was also able to appeal to the doctrine of double effect, arguing that her intention had been to relieve her mother's suffering, not to cause her death. Although her arguments were largely accepted by the court, she was nonetheless convicted on the grounds that the morphine dose she administered exceeded the level necessary to control her mother's suffering. She received a conditional jail sentence of one week plus one year's probation.

The *Postma* case ignited a lively debate in the Netherlands concerning the conditions under which euthanasia might be justified. The subsequent course of that debate and of the development of Dutch policy on PAD were shaped primarily by three influences: standards of medical practice developed by the Royal Dutch Medical Association (RDMA), recommendations of official government commissions, and further court decisions. As early as 1975 the RDMA adopted the position that, under certain circumstances, PAE could be considered to be standard medical practice. That position then played an important role in the *Schoonheim* case in the early 1980s. In July 1982 Dr. Schoonheim administered a lethal injection to Caroline B., a ninety-five-year-old patient who was chronically, though not terminally, ill and who wished to die before developing further problems that would impair her ability to make decisions for herself. After discussing the matter with a colleague and with Ms. B.'s son, Dr. Schoonheim decided to administer euthanasia. Like Dr. Postma, he then notified the authorities and, like her, was charged. At his trial in April 1983 Dr. Schoonheim's defense of necessity was rejected by the court, a decision that was upheld by the Court of Appeals. However, when it heard the case in November 1984 the Supreme Court concluded that the necessity defense had not been adequately considered by the lower courts. The case was sent back to the Court of Appeals, which asked the RDMA whether current ethical norms could justify euthanasia in cases of conflict of duty. When the RDMA replied in the affirmative the court acquitted Dr. Schoonheim.[13]

The *Schoonheim* case established that physicians could appeal to necessity in order to justify euthanasia. However, it did not set out clear guidelines for determining when the defense of necessity would apply. In order to fill this gap, in 1984 the RDMA released a report on the "requirements of careful practice" for all cases of "conduct that is intended to terminate another person's life at his or her explicit request"—thus covering both PAE and PAS.[14] Besides stipulating that these acts could be carried out only by a physician, the RDMA laid out five conditions: (1) the patient's request must be competent, voluntary, explicit, and persistent; (2) it must be based on full information; (3) the patient must be in a situation of intolerable and hopeless suffering; (4) there must be no acceptable alternative means of alleviating this suffering; and (5) the physician involved must consult at least one colleague whose judgment can be expected to be independent.

These conditions quickly became the unofficial guidelines for prosecutors in deciding whether to lay charges since they furnished a basis for estimating the likelihood of conviction. In Dutch criminal law prosecutorial decision-making is centralized in the national Board of Procurators General. Once the conditions articulated by the RDMA were adopted by the board, physicians who adhered to them could have a reasonable expectation of escaping prosecution. In this way, though euthanasia and assisted suicide both remained *de jure* prohibited under the Dutch Criminal Code, they were *de facto* permitted as long as the RDMA guidelines were observed.

By the early 1990s most of the essential elements of the Dutch policy on PAD were in place, though largely in the shape of guidelines for prosecution under the existing Criminal Code statutes. One of those elements was that though patients need not be diagnosed with a terminal condition, they must be experiencing suffering variously characterized as "unacceptable," "intolerable," or "hopeless and unbearable." It was clear that these formulae were meant to apply to physical suffering but less clear that they might also encompass psychological or emotional suffering with no organic basis. This aspect of the guidelines was addressed in the case of Dr. Boudewijn Chabot, a psychiatrist who in September 1991 supplied his fifty-year-old patient Hilly Bosscher with lethal medication at her request. Ms. Bosscher had endured extreme depression for a number of years after the failure of her marriage and the deaths of her two sons (both at age twenty), but she was by all accounts physically healthy. She had rejected all offers of palliative care and was steadfast in her desire to die. At his 1993 trial for assisting a suicide Dr. Chabot invoked the defense of necessity, a defense that the court accepted, noting explicitly that it was equally available in cases in which the patient's suffering is psychological rather than physical. When this verdict was appealed in 1994, the Supreme Court affirmed that necessity can apply to cases of nonsomatic suffering. In light of the *Chabot* decision, the minister of justice announced that henceforth physical suffering would no longer be required for immunity from prosecution, and charges were dropped against eleven physicians who had assisted the deaths of mentally ill patients.[15]

Later in the decade the case of Dr. Philip Sutorius threatened to push the envelope even further by eliminating the suffering requirement entirely. In April 1998 Dr. Sutorius assisted the suicide of Edward Brongersma, an eighty-six-year-old former senator. Senator Brongersma suffered from no physical or mental illness; his reasons for wanting to die were concern about further physical decline, a feeling that his existence was hopeless, and a general "tiredness of life." Dr. Sutorius's acquittal at his 2000 trial was appealed by the minister of justice and subsequently overturned in 2001 by the Court of Appeals, which held that the patient's suffering must be of a medical (physical or psychological), and not merely an "existential," nature. This ruling was affirmed by the Supreme Court in 2002.[16]

Throughout the 1980s and 1990s various attempts were made to amend the Dutch Criminal Code so as to bring its provisions concerning assisted death into line with the *de facto* policy governing prosecution. These efforts finally yielded results when the Termination of Life on Request and Assisted Suicide (Review Procedures) Act passed both houses in the Dutch Parliament and came into effect in April 2002. The legislation introduced exceptions to the Criminal Code articles governing both PAS and PAE, stipulating that these acts not be punishable when both the requirements of due care and the notification procedure have been observed. The due care criteria laid out in the act required that the attending physician (a) be satisfied that the patient has made a voluntary, explicit, and carefully considered request; (b) be satisfied that the patient's suffering is unbearable and that there is no prospect of improvement; (c) have informed the patient about his or her situation and prospects; (d) have come to the conclusion, together with the patient, that there is no reasonable alternative in the light of the patient's condition; (e) have consulted at least one other, independent, physician, who must have seen the patient and given a written opinion on the due care criteria in (a)–(d); and (f) exercise due medical care and attention in terminating the patient's life or providing assistance with the patient's suicide. The legislation also made provision for PAD in the case of currently incompetent (but formerly competent) patients who had included such a request in their advance directive. Finally, the due care criteria were also stipulated to apply to "mature minors" between the ages of twelve and eighteen as long as they were "deemed to be capable of making a reasonable appraisal of their own interests" and their parents or guardians either had been consulted (ages sixteen to eighteen) or had consented (ages twelve to sixteen).[17]

In addition to formally legalizing PAD (subject to the requirements of due care), the legislation laid out a new notification procedure by establishing regional review committees. In a case of PAD the physician is not permitted to issue a natural death certificate. Instead, the physician must notify the municipal pathologist of the cause of death and complete a standard form detailing whether and how the requirements of due care were met. The pathologist then completes a form notifying the regional review committee and forwards the physician's report. The committee makes a determination of whether the due care criteria have been satisfied. If so, then no further action is taken; if not, then the committee must inform the Board of Procurators General, which makes the decision whether to initiate a prosecution. The regional review committees are intended to serve as a buffer between physicians and justice officials so that only in exceptional cases need prosecutors be involved in cases of PAD. There are currently five such committees, whose jurisdiction is divided geographically, each of which is mandated to make an annual report to the government concerning its caseload for the year.

With the enactment of the Law on Euthanasia in September 2002, Belgium became the second jurisdiction to legalize PAE. The Belgian legislation was clearly influenced by, and to a considerable extent modeled after, the Dutch law, which came into effect in the same year. However, the process leading to its adoption was very different, and the law itself departed from its Dutch counterpart in several significant respects. As we have seen, the Dutch law essentially codified preexisting practice, which had developed gradually over a period of three decades, shaped by case law, medical opinion, and government reports. Virtually none of those preconditions were in place in Belgium. There was little debate about euthanasia in that country prior to 1995 and no case law to fall back on since there had been virtually no prosecutions for mercy killing. Furthermore, no medical association in the country had taken the position that euthanasia could be accepted medical treatment or meet the "requirements of careful practice." If the Dutch process leading to formal decriminalization was a bottom-up one, the corresponding Belgian process was very much top-down.

During the 1980s and 1990s several euthanasia bills had been submitted to the Belgian Parliament with no success. The issue began to gain traction in 1996 when the presidents of the Senate and the House of Representatives made a joint request to the newly established Belgian Advisory Committee on Bioethics for advice on whether euthanasia should be legalized. The committee responded in 1997 with its Advice No. 1 Concerning the Desirability of a Legal Recognition of Euthanasia. The terms of reference for the committee stipulated that its reports must reflect the diversity of public opinion on the topic in question. Instead of formulating a recommendation concerning euthanasia, therefore, the committee outlined four possible ways of proceeding, ranging from outright decriminalization to outright prohibition, with the Dutch policy as one intermediary option. As we will see, the legislation eventually adopted in 2002 essentially took up this last option (with some important modifications). Meanwhile, in 1999 the committee produced its second report on end-of-life issues: Advice No. 9 Concerning Termination of Life of Incompetent Patients. The second report was necessary since for its first report the committee had adopted the Dutch definition of euthanasia as "the intentional termination of life on request"; questions of (what we would call) nonvoluntary euthanasia of incompetent patients (such as infants) therefore required separate treatment. True to its mandate, the committee once again limited itself to outlining different possible legal regimes ranging this time from partial decriminalization to outright prohibition.

The Belgian Law on Euthanasia also adopted the Dutch definition; it therefore did not deal with nonvoluntary euthanasia, and no official action has been taken in Belgium to date on that front. In a number of respects the law mirrored the Dutch legislation. It set out the conditions under which euthanasia administered by a physician would not constitute a criminal offense, including the following: (a) a legally competent patient must make a voluntary, well-considered, and durable request; (b) the patient must be in a medically futile condition of constant and unbearable physical or mental suffering that cannot be alleviated in any other way; (c) the patient must be fully informed about his or her diagnosis, prognosis, and alternative treatment options; and (d) a second, independent physician must be consulted, and that physician must also examine the patient.

As in the Netherlands, the Belgian law focused on suffering and did not require the patient to be in a terminal condition. However, if the patient's condition is not terminal, then the attending physician must consult yet another physician "who is a psychiatrist or specialist in the disorder in question." The law also explicitly allowed for "euthanasia directives"—advance directives in which PAE is requested under certain specified circumstances—but stated that they can be triggered only by the complete unconsciousness of the patient and not by other conditions, such as dementia. Finally, the law stipulated a notification procedure with various documents to be completed by the physician and forwarded to the Federal Control and Evaluation Commission. The task of the commission is to satisfy itself that each case has conformed to the conditions of the legislation; if it is not satisfied, then it is to turn the case over to the public prosecutor. It is also mandated to publish biannual statistical reports on the operation of the legislation.

Despite these similarities, however, the Belgian law also contained some noteworthy departures from its Dutch counterpart. The most striking is the absence of any mention of PAS. This omission may be due to the fact that, unlike the Dutch Criminal Code, the Belgian Penal Code does not explicitly prohibit assisting a suicide. Whatever the reason, the law's silence concerning PAS struck many commentators as anomalous, since if euthanasia is accepted as lawful (under appropriate conditions), how can assisted suicide not be accepted as well? The anomaly was addressed in 2004 by the Federal Control and Evaluation Commission, which stated that it would consider PAS to fall within the definition of PAE.

The 2002 law required that patients requesting euthanasia be adults or "emancipated minors"—basically, minors who are independent of their parents (for example, due to marriage). It therefore did not apply to other "mature minors" (between the ages of twelve and eighteen). However, in 2014 it was amended to permit terminally ill children to request euthanasia if they are near death, suffering "constant and unbearable physical" pain with no available treatment, and fully able to understand the implications of their decision. The consent of the parents would be necessary, as would that of a medical team, including a psychiatrist. Belgium is now the only jurisdiction in the world to have no stipulated minimum age limit for PAD.

In Luxembourg a bill to legalize both euthanasia and assisted suicide passed into law in March 2009, completing the Benelux sweep. The passage of the bill occasioned a minor constitutional crisis since the Grand Duke Henri, whose assent was necessary in order for any bill to become law, indicated in December that he would refuse assent to the bill. As a result, the legislature voted to limit his constitutional power to promulgating, rather than approving, legislation. Most of the provisions of the Luxembourg legislation (both substantive and procedural) closely followed the Belgian law, except for the fact that PAS was explicitly covered as well as PAE and the law applied to mature minors between the ages of sixteen and eighteen, who may request PAD with the permission of their parents or guardians. Both of these provisions moved the legislation a little closer to the Dutch model.

The first country outside Europe to legalize PAE was Colombia, whose Constitutional Court struck down the prohibition of euthanasia in May 1997. Ironically, the case had been brought to the court by euthanasia opponents who wished to strengthen the existing law regarding "mercy killing"; instead, to their dismay, it was dismantled by a 6–3 majority on the grounds that it violated constitutional guarantees of autonomy and dignity. The effect of the decision was to decriminalize voluntary euthanasia when practiced by physicians. (Interestingly, the decision left the criminal prohibition of assisting a suicide in place.) The court suggested the sorts of guidelines that would need to be put in place to regulate the practice but left their implementation to Congress. For nearly twenty years the legislators failed to rise to this challenge. Finally, in February 2015 the court ordered the country's Ministry of Health to establish a protocol for access to PAE. Under the new regulations, which came into effect in April 2015, hospitals are required to set up committees to evaluate requests for PAE. Access is restricted to adults with terminal illnesses such as cancer. Patients with neurodegenerative illnesses are excluded. However, the regulations permit PAE for patients who are unconscious if relatives can provide proof of an advance request for it.

The most recent jurisdiction to take the step to legalization has been Canada. In 1993 the section of the Canadian Criminal Code that prohibited assisted suicide was challenged on constitutional grounds by Sue Rodriguez, who was diagnosed in her early forties with ALS. Foreseeing that the relentless progress of the disease would eventually render her unable to swallow, speak, move, or breathe on her own, she wished to choose the time and manner of her death by a lethal dose of medication. However, she knew that when that time arrived she would need the assistance of a physician. Unwilling to ask any physician to commit an unlawful act, she decided to challenge the law on the grounds that it violated her rights to equality and to liberty and security of the person under the Canadian Charter of Rights and Freedoms. Her challenge was unsuccessful in both the trial court and the British Columbia Court of Appeal. On further appeal, the Supreme Court was deeply divided on the case, with a narrow majority of 5–4 finding against the challenge.[18] Although the legal issue had been decided, at least for a time, Rodriguez herself was determined to follow through with her wishes. In February 1994 she obtained a prescription for secobarbital from an unknown physician and died peacefully in her home, accompanied only by Svend Robinson, a member of Parliament. No one was ever charged with involvement in her death.

In the years that followed, various private members' bills aiming to legalize PAD were debated in the Canadian Parliament, but none came close to adoption. There matters rested until a new constitutional challenge was launched in 2011 by the British Columbia Civil Liberties Association, this time targeting the Criminal Code sections prohibiting both PAS and PAE. The plaintiffs in the action included a married couple, Lee Carter and Hollis Johnson, who in 2010 had accompanied Carter's mother Kay to Switzerland for an assisted death through Dignitas. Kay Carter had suffered serious pain and disability due to spinal stenosis, an incurable degenerative condition that results in severe nerve compression in the spine. But the most prominent plaintiff was a woman in her sixties named Gloria Taylor who, like Sue Rodriguez, had ALS and wished to be able to control the manner and timing of her death.

The case was argued before Madame Justice Lynn Smith of the British Columbia Supreme Court in November 2011. In June 2012 Justice Smith handed down her decision.[19] In a lengthy and closely argued judgment she found that the prohibition of both PAS and PAE violated the plaintiffs' constitutional rights to equality and to life, liberty, and security of the person. Her key finding was that a blanket ban on these practices was overbroad since the experience of other jurisdictions had shown that a carefully regulated regime could adequately protect vulnerable persons while also providing access to PAD for patients seeking relief from needless suffering. She therefore struck down the impugned sections of the Criminal Code as constitutionally invalid. She also granted Gloria Taylor a constitutional exemption during this period so that she could seek PAD. However, Taylor never came to exercise this right; only four months later she died of an infection.

Inevitably, the trial judge's decision was appealed to the Supreme Court. In its February 2015 judgment the court unanimously struck down the blanket ban on PAD, primarily on grounds of overbreadth.[20] Like Justice Smith, the court found that adequate safeguards could protect the vulnerable while permitting access to PAD for those in need of it. That access, the court ruled, had to be provided to any "competent adult person who (1) clearly consents to the termination of life; and (2) has a grievous and irremediable medical condition (including an illness, disease, or disability) that causes enduring suffering that is intolerable to the individual in the circumstances of his or her condition." The court suspended its judgment for a year in order to provide both the federal government and the provincial and territorial governments time to formulate more narrowly targeted legislation with an appropriate regulatory framework. The period of suspension was later extended by an additional four months.

Meanwhile, during the time that the *Carter* case was working its way through the judicial system, the province of Quebec decided to go its own way with PAD. On the basis that the regulation of medical services falls under provincial responsibility for health care, the Quebec National Assembly passed the Act Respecting End-of-Life Care in June 2014. As the title of the legislation suggests, it dealt broadly with end-of-life issues, including palliative care and terminal sedation. But it also permitted "medical aid in dying" in the case of a free and informed request by a competent adult who (1) suffers from a serious and incurable illness, (2) is in an advanced state of irreversible decline in capability, and (3) experiences constant and unbearable physical or psychological suffering that cannot be relieved in a manner the patient deems tolerable. The legislation had the usual safeguards, including a confirming opinion by a second independent physician and review of all cases of PAD by a provincial oversight body. The act came into force in January 2016.

The federal legislation mandated by the *Carter* decision was finally passed by the Canadian Parliament in June 2016.[21] Unlike the Quebec law, what it labeled "medical assistance in dying" encompassed both PAS and PAE. Whereas the Supreme Court had left "adult" undefined, the legislation stipulated a minimum age of eighteen, thus making no provision for mature minors. It also required that patients reaffirm their "express consent" at the time that PAD is administered, thereby excluding advance requests. For the most part, the qualifying criteria for PAD reflected those laid down by the court, including the requirement that the patient's medical condition "causes them enduring physical or psychological suffering that is intolerable to them and that cannot be relieved under conditions that they consider acceptable." In this respect the legislation resembled the laws in place in the Benelux countries. On the other hand, however, the requirement that patients have a "grievous and irremediable medical condition" was qualified significantly by adding the provision that they be "in an advanced state of irreversible decline in capability" (a condition taken over from the Quebec law) and that "their natural death has become reasonably foreseeable, taking into account all of their medical circumstances, without a prognosis necessarily having been made as to the specific length of time that they have remaining." Although these qualifications are rather vague, they seem intended to require that patients be in a terminal condition. They also seem intended to exclude patients presenting solely with psychiatric conditions, regardless of how otherwise "grievous and irremediable" those conditions might be or how much physical or psychological suffering they might cause.

Because these qualifications will have the effect of excluding some patients who would have satisfied the *Carter* criteria, both the Quebec and Canadian laws may be vulnerable to constitutional challenge. The Quebec law may be additionally vulnerable because it permits only PAE and not PAS. Therefore, while a legal regime for PAD is now in place in Canada, its final shape may not be determined for some time to come.

What has been happening in the United States?

Until 1997 PAD remained a criminal offense in all fifty states. The best-known advocate for legalization was Dr. Jack Kevorkian, who between 1990 and 1998 assisted the suicides of more than one hundred clients who sought out his services. During this time he was prosecuted on several occasions in Michigan but never convicted. However, in September 1998 he administered (voluntary) euthanasia to a fifty-two-year-old man who was in the final stages of ALS. Dr. Kevorkian then allowed a videotape he had made of this episode to be aired on the CBS newsmagazine *60 Minutes*, during which he dared the authorities to prosecute him. He got his wish in March 1999 when he was charged with first-degree murder and the delivery of a controlled substance (administering a lethal injection). The law on homicide being much more settled in the state of Michigan than that of assisted suicide, he was convicted of second-degree murder and sentenced to a period of ten to twenty-five years in prison. In June 2007 he was paroled for good behavior and died four years later of complications arising from liver cancer.

During the 1990s the laws prohibiting PAS in the states of Washington and New York were challenged in cases that reached the US Supreme Court.[22] In its 1997 *Glucksberg* decision the court ruled that the right to assistance in suicide is not a fundamental liberty interest protected by the due process clause of the Fourteenth Amendment. Furthermore, it found that Washington's ban on assisting a suicide was rationally related to various important state interests, including the preservation of life and the protection of vulnerable groups, and that legalizing assisted suicide would set the law on a "slippery slope" toward the legalization of euthanasia. In the companion case of *Quill* the court determined that the New York law did not offend against the equal protection clause of the Fourteenth Amendment by drawing an arbitrary distinction between assistance in suicide and refusal of life-sustaining treatment.

Since those decisions, PAS has become legally available in six US states. Oregon was the first American jurisdiction to enact legislation legalizing any form of PAD. In November 1994 voters in Oregon passed Ballot Measure 16—the Oregon Death with Dignity Act (ODDA)—by a margin of 51% to 49%. (For the text of the act, see the Appendix.) The effect of the ODDA was to legalize PAS—but not PAE—under carefully controlled conditions. A group of doctors, patients, and nursing homes in Oregon immediately filed a class action complaint against the state.

In December 1994 the Oregon Federal District Court issued a preliminary injunction against the act, and in August 1995 it made the injunction permanent. In February 1997 the Ninth Circuit Court reversed this injunction on the grounds that the complainants did not have standing since they faced no infringement of life or liberty under the act. When the Supreme Court refused to review this decision, the state legislature put Measure 51, which would have repealed the ODDA, on the ballot for the November 1997 election. The citizens of Oregon reaffirmed the act, this time by a margin of 60% to 40%.

The ODDA has been in force in Oregon since 1997 and during that time has survived one further legal challenge. In November 2001 US Attorney General John Ashcroft issued an interpretative rule to the federal Drug Enforcement Administration (DEA) stating that PAS is not a legitimate purpose for prescribing medication regulated by the Controlled Substances Act. Under this rule physicians in Oregon who prescribe for this purpose could have their DEA registrations suspended, regardless of the ODDA, so that they would no longer be able to prescribe controlled substances. In April 2002 a US District Court issued a permanent injunction against the Ashcroft rule. This injunction was upheld by the Ninth Circuit Court in May 2004 and then by the US Supreme Court in January 2006.[23] When this decision by the Supreme Court is combined with its 1997 decisions in *Glucksberg* and *Quill* the net result is that states are constitutionally permitted to legalize PAS but not required to do so.

Many of the provisions in the ODDA will by now be familiar: patient decisional capacity; a voluntary, informed, and repeated request; consultation with a second physician. All cases falling under the act must be documented and reported to the Oregon Public Health Division. However, in certain important respects the Oregon policy stakes out its own distinctive ground. Unlike the three Benelux countries, Colombia, and Canada, it permits only PAS, not PAE. But unlike Switzerland, it allows no official role for private right-to-die organizations in the process; PAS is to be both provided by and reported by physicians. The ODDA applies only to adults (eighteen years of age or older), making no provision for "mature" or "emancipated" minors. It also requires patients to be legal residents of the state. More significantly, the act requires patients to have been diagnosed with a terminal disease, defined as "an incurable and irreversible disease that has been medically confirmed and will, within reasonable medical judgment, produce death within six months." There is no requirement of suffering, "unbearable" or otherwise. The Oregon policy therefore inverts the eligibility criteria in the European jurisdictions, all of which require suffering and none of which require a terminal condition. In this respect it is simultaneously more permissive and more restrictive than these other policies.

In November 2008, when voters approved Ballot Initiative I-1000 by a wide margin of 58% to 42%, Washington became the second state in the union to legalize PAS. The legislation came into effect in March 2009, and the first assisted suicide under the terms of the law took place in May of the same year. With only one or two relatively minor variations, the Washington Death with Dignity Act is a clause-by-clause copy of its Oregon counterpart. As in Oregon, the Washington legislation does not refer to the practice it authorizes as "assisted suicide" but rather as "death with dignity" or "self-administering medication to end one's life in a humane and dignified manner."[24] Both statutes contain clauses stating that the practice authorized by their provisions does not constitute suicide or assisted suicide, and the Washington law explicitly prohibits the mandated annual reports by the Department of Health from referring to this practice in this way; it further requires that the cause of death be reported as the patient's "underlying terminal disease." The terminological issue featured prominently in preelection discussions of initiative I-1000, with opponents of the measure insisting that it would legalize assisted suicide while proponents preferred the blander language of death with dignity. The issue was driven primarily by the social stigma attached to suicide. The annual reports issued for the first eight years of the Oregon policy used the language of PAS. This practice was abandoned in 2006, largely at the behest of families and right-to-die organizations.

In December 2008 Montana became the only American jurisdiction to legalize PAS by judicial, rather than legislative, means. Judge McCarter of the First Judicial District Court ruled that the state's prohibition of PAS violated rights to individual privacy and dignity guaranteed by the state constitution. In the following month Judge McCarter denied a request by the Montana attorney general's office that her ruling be stayed. Upon appeal by the attorney general, in December 2009 a divided Montana Supreme Court overruled Judge McCarter's constitutional decision but also found that nothing in state law prohibited assisting a suicide.[25] That ruling shields doctors from prosecution as long as they have the patient's request in writing. It is, of course, open to the Montana state legislature to close that legal loophole. Until it chooses to do so, Montana arguably has the most liberal assisted suicide policy in the country since no legislative guidelines have yet been enacted to regulate it. Judge McCarter's ruling specified only three requirements: that the patient must be mentally competent and terminally ill and that the physician's involvement in the treatment must be limited to prescribing the lethal medication, rather than administering it.

In May 2013 Vermont became the first state to pass legislation allowing PAD without having the bill first approved in a ballot initiative. The Patient Choice and Control at End of Life Act largely adopted the Oregon model, with its restriction to PAS and to patients diagnosed with a terminal illness. Although all cases must be reported to the state Department of Health, no particular oversight body was established to monitor compliance. Beginning in 2018 the department is mandated to start issuing biennial statistical reports based on the cases reported to it.

California then followed the same route in September 2015, when the legislature passed the End of Life Option Act, which Governor Jerry Brown then signed and which went into effect in June 2016. Passage of the California law was almost certainly influenced by the extensive publicity surrounding Brittany Maynard, who in April 2014 was diagnosed with stage 4 glioblastoma, a highly aggressive and usually fatal form of brain cancer, and given a life expectancy of less than six months. Maynard was determined to die on her own terms. Since PAS was not legal at that time in her home state of California, she decided to move to Portland, Oregon, to establish residency so that she could take advantage of the provisions of the ODDA. During her time there she joined Compassion and Choices and launched an advocacy campaign for the legalization of PAS, including a video that has been viewed more than 12 million times. Her assisted death took place in November 2014, just before her thirtieth birthday.

Finally, in November 2016 voters in Colorado approved the End of Life Options Act by ballot initiative. As in the other states, the act is closely modeled on the ODDA. At the time of writing, bills to legalize PAS are at various stages of consideration in the legislatures of nearly half of the states, plus the District of Columbia.

6

WHAT ARE THE OPTIONS FOR A LEGAL REGIME?

Must the illness be terminal?

The historical sketch in the previous chapter should make it clear that policies of legal physician-assisted death can come in various shapes and sizes. The legal regime in place in Switzerland differs in many respects from that of the Benelux countries, which differs in turn from that of the American states. The fact is that in crafting a policy of legal PAD there are many decisions to be made, such that two policies can end up quite dissimilar from one another. In this chapter we will consider these decision points systematically so as to have a better sense of the range of options available. In doing so, we will keep only two factors constant. First, we will continue to deal only with voluntary PAD, in which the service is requested by a contemporaneously competent patient. We will consider the further complications occasioned by nonvoluntary PAD later (in Chapter 9). Second, we will continue to assume that the policy authorizes death to be assisted only by a physician, thus that we are dealing with *physician-assisted death*. We will not consider the legality of suicides being assisted by laypersons, such as family or friends.

Under the Oregon Death with Dignity Act patients can qualify for PAD only if they have been diagnosed with a terminal illness, defined as "an incurable and irreversible disease that has been medically confirmed and will, within reasonable medical judgment, produce death within six months." This choice of a six-month horizon was prompted by the state eligibility conditions for admission to hospice care and was incorporated as well into the policies adopted subsequently in Washington, Vermont, California, and Colorado. The policy in Colombia likewise requires a terminal diagnosis, while the law in Quebec somewhat more vaguely restricts PAD to patients in "an advanced state of irreversible decline in capability." The Canadian law adds to this the similarly vague requirement that the patient's natural death have become "reasonably foreseeable." On the other hand, there is no similar restriction in the Dutch policy (or in the other Benelux countries); instead, it is enough that the patient have a medical condition that is causing "unbearable suffering with no prospect of improvement."

This decision point marks a major difference between the Oregon and Dutch models for access to legal PAD. The absence of a suffering requirement from the Oregon policy is perhaps understandable since the prospect of having no more than six months to live may be assumed itself to cause considerable distress, in addition to whatever physical symptoms accompany the patient's illness (which, in the great majority of cases, is cancer). On the other hand, the Dutch focus on suffering may explain the absence of the terminal diagnosis requirement since any illness that will continue to cause unbearable suffering for more than six months, with no prospect of improvement, could be considered to present an even more irrefutable case for PAD. Of course, in the broadest sense virtually all patients who satisfy the suffering requirement will be afflicted with some condition that will (sooner or later) be fatal. In this sense, therefore, a requirement of a terminal diagnosis might be redundant. But if the requirement is drawn more narrowly, as it is in Oregon, then it would appear to be inconsistent with the spirit of the Dutch policy, whose purpose seems to be to enable patients to avoid unnecessary suffering.

The terminal diagnosis requirement, with its six-month horizon, has the advantage of being more or less objective, based as it is on medical judgment concerning the patient's prognosis. The requirement of "unbearable suffering," on the other hand, is inevitably subjective since each patient must decide his or her own tolerance level for the symptoms accompanying the medical condition. What one person finds unbearable another may elect to bear. Under these regimes, therefore, the primary criterion of eligibility for PAD lies very much in the patient's hands, rather than in the medical judgment of the attending physician. On the other hand, we should not exaggerate the objectivity of the terminal diagnosis condition. The six-month horizon represents the attending physician's educated forecast of the patient's survival prospects, and it can turn out to be either an over- or an underestimate. In Oregon, which requires the six-month horizon, some patients who have elected PAS have lived well beyond that deadline before using their prescribed medication. The six-month limit can also appear quite arbitrary. It will be a reasonable fit for many (perhaps most) cancer cases, though not for all. But it applies less readily to neurodegenerative conditions such as amyotrophic lateral sclerosis, which are invariably fatal but may take much longer to run their course. In these cases, requiring a patient to wait to make a request for PAD until death can be confidently predicted within six months seems a needless bureaucratic nicety.

The terminal diagnosis requirement will also exclude PAD for patients who are suffering from serious, long-standing, but nonterminal conditions such as total-body paralysis. We met one such patient, Nancy B., in the previous chapter. As it happened, since her condition rendered her dependent on a ventilator, she was able to hasten her death by requesting its removal. But otherwise she would have been compelled to continue what she regarded as an intolerable existence since her ventilator and feeding tubes could keep her alive indefinitely (she had already been in this condition for two and a half years before she refused further life support). An Englishman named Tony Nicklinson was less fortunate. A catastrophic stroke suffered in 2005 left him with locked-in syndrome: paralyzed from the neck down and without the ability to speak. He described his life following the stroke as a "living nightmare" and in 2012 petitioned the UK courts for the right to PAD. When his petition was refused, Nicklinson began to decline food and water and died of pneumonia six days after the court decision. The United Kingdom, of course, has no policy of legal PAD, but Nicklinson would have been equally out of luck in Oregon since he could not satisfy the six-month requirement.

So the first, and in many ways most basic, decision a policy of legal PAD must make is whether to foreground length of life (terminal diagnosis) or quality of life (unbearable suffering). Many patients, especially end-stage cancer patients, will of course qualify under either type of regime. But not all.

What kinds of suffering should be recognized?

A policy, like the one in the Netherlands, that elects to incorporate a condition of "unbearable suffering" will then face questions about the types of suffering that might qualify. No one doubts that suffering due to such physical symptoms as pain, nausea, dizziness, or shortness of

breath will suffice, if it rises to a level the patient deems unbearable or intolerable. However, as related in the previous
chapter, it has been clear in the Netherlands since the 1994
Chabot decision that psychological suffering may qualify as
well. This provision was then explicitly incorporated into
the Belgian Euthanasia Act of 2002, which requires that the
patient be in "a medically futile condition of constant and
unbearable physical or mental suffering."[1] Both physical
and psychological suffering are also explicitly recognized
in the Canadian law.

The category of psychological suffering will certainly
include forms of distress accompanying psychiatric conditions, such as chronic depression or personality disorders.
However, we will consider in the next section whether
patients presenting solely or primarily with psychiatric
illnesses should qualify for PAD. Meanwhile, it will suffice to note that psychological, or psychosocial, suffering may motivate requests for PAD by patients whose
underlying illness is strictly physical. The Oregon Public
Health Division publishes an annual statistical report on
the operation of the Death with Dignity Act. This report
breaks down the number of patients who have utilized
the provisions of the act in the previous calendar year
along several dimensions: sex, age, race, underlying illness, etc. It also lists these patients' end-of-life concerns,
the ones that motivated them to seek an assisted suicide.
Inadequate pain control is one item on this list, but it is
cited by only about a quarter of patients. Much more frequently cited are, in rank order, such forms of psychological distress as loss of autonomy, diminished ability to
engage in the activities that make life enjoyable, loss of
dignity, and concern about being a burden on family or
caregivers.

However, considered as evidence of the kinds of suffering that motivate patient requests for physician-assisted

suicide in Oregon, the annual reports have some significant drawbacks. Principal among them is the fact that those concerns are not voiced directly by the patients themselves. The Oregon law requires patients to submit a written "Request for Medication to End My Life in a Humane and Dignified Manner." However, it does not require them to provide any reason for this request. For any patient who dies as a result of ingesting the medication, the attending physician must submit a follow-up report that records, *inter alia*, the concerns that motivated the request. For this the physician is given a checklist of the aforementioned concerns, each of which requires a response of "Yes," "No," or "Don't Know." What we have in the annual reports, therefore, is an aggregate of the motivating reasons that doctors attribute to their patients on the basis of whatever direct information they might have, these reasons being selected from a predetermined list.

Fortunately, we can do a little better. Since its inception in 1997 the operation of the Oregon Death with Dignity Act has been extensively studied by Dr. Linda Ganzini and her colleagues. In 2008 Ganzini published the results of a survey in which she asked family members of decedents who had requested PAD to rank twenty-eight possible reasons their loved ones made the request.[2] The authors' apparent assumption was that family members might have more intimate knowledge of the patient's motives and values than did the attending health care professionals. Of the twenty-eight possible reasons, current physical symptoms such as pain ranked quite low, though concern about future symptoms ranked somewhat higher. But the most frequently cited reasons were such "existential" factors as wanting to control the circumstances of death and fear of loss of dignity or independence. These results were then replicated in a 2009 study in which Ganzini and colleagues applied the same methodology to persons who had either requested PAD or contacted an advocacy organization (Compassion and Choices of Oregon) for information about the process.[3]

It seems safe to conclude, therefore, that psychological distress plays a prominent role alongside physical suffering in motivating decisions by patients to seek PAD. If this is the case, then it would seem arbitrary to exclude it as a qualifying factor for access. If the decision is once made to focus on suffering as a criterion, as opposed to projected life expectancy, then it looks as though all forms of suffering must matter.

What kinds of illnesses should be included?

The inclusion of psychological suffering, however, raises the question of whether it can stand alone as a qualifying factor for PAD. One of the implications of the Oregon requirement of a terminal diagnosis is that all patients requesting PAD in that state will present with a physical illness. The illness may (and almost certainly will) cause both physical and psychological suffering, but it will itself be physical. Among the data summarized in the Oregon annual reports are the underlying illnesses of the patients requesting (and receiving) PAD. Cancer is the overwhelmingly most frequent diagnosis (nearly 80%), followed by neurodegenerative diseases such as ALS (10%), chronic lower respiratory disease (5%), heart disease (3%), HIV/AIDS (1%), and a variety of other illnesses making up the remaining 1%. Cases in which patients present either solely or primarily with a psychiatric illness, such as chronic depression or personality disorder, simply do not occur, presumably because they are never diagnosed as terminal. The same would appear to be true in Canada, where the law requires that the patient's natural death be "reasonably foreseeable."

Predictably, the situation is different in jurisdictions that require "unbearable suffering" but not a terminal diagnosis. If psychological (or "existential") suffering counts, then there will inevitably be cases in which it stems from a mental rather than a physical illness. In these cases there is no reason to exclude the possibility that the suffering could be "unbearable" or that, if it has been refractory to treatment, there might be "no prospect of improvement." The annual reports issued by the Dutch Regional Euthanasia Review Committees also list the underlying illnesses of patients who have received PAD. As in Oregon, cancer is by far the most frequent diagnosis (about 75% of all cases), followed by neurological disorders and cardiovascular disease. However, unlike Oregon, a small percentage of illnesses (less than 1%) are recorded as psychiatric in nature. The situation is much the same in Belgium, except that the incidence of psychiatric cases there appears to be a little higher (about 3%–4%). Many of these patients in both jurisdictions present with comorbidities—that is, physical illnesses in addition to their psychiatric condition. For some, however, the psychiatric diagnosis stands alone.

The case for including psychiatric illnesses in the eligibility criteria for PAD echoes the case for including psychological suffering: if all suffering should count, then so should all illness. More particularly, if it can be possible for the suffering accompanying a psychiatric illness to rise to the level of being "unbearable," then it can also be possible for the illness itself to have "no prospect of improvement." In that case, it would appear discriminatory to exclude psychiatric conditions as a category.

However, their inclusion does raise some special difficulties. For one thing, many psychiatric conditions, such as depressive disorders, may have a distorting effect on decision-making, challenging the requirement that patients be decisionally capable. This issue was confronted by the Dutch Supreme Court in the 1994 *Chabot* case and by the Swiss Federal Tribunal in the 2006 case of X. Y. (both discussed in the previous chapter). In each case the court concluded that while a serious psychiatric disorder may impair decisional capacity, it need not do so. Psychiatric patients, therefore, could not be excluded from requesting PAD simply on the grounds that their illness is mental rather than physical. However, the courts also recognized that special care needs to be taken in these cases to ensure that the patient is capable of making a clear and informed decision for PAD. This might, for instance, call for an additional level of scrutiny for competency (a possibility to be discussed below).

The second complication arising in psychiatric cases concerns the requirement that the illness be incurable or untreatable. The Dutch law, as we have seen, requires that there be "no prospect of improvement," while the Belgian law speaks of the patient having a "serious and incurable disorder" and being in a "medically futile condition." The criteria laid down by the Canadian Supreme Court in its *Carter* decision similarly specify a "grievous and irremediable" medical condition, and the law in Quebec stipulates "an incurable serious illness." Part of the difficulty is in the determination of when a psychiatric condition has become "incurable" or "irremediable," though it should be noted that in the Dutch cases most of the patients had been under treatment for years, in some instances as long as thirty years.[4] Under the guidelines of the Dutch Psychiatric Association, treatment for a mental disorder must meet three conditions: (1) it must offer a real prospect of improvement, (2) it must be possible to administer within a reasonable period of time, and (3) there must be a reasonable balance between its expected benefits and burdens for the patient. Whether a condition is "incurable" or whether a treatment is "medically futile" is therefore a complex matter involving both professional judgment and the values of the patient. This judgment call is complicated even further by the fact that the patient has the right to refuse any and all treatment. That right was explicitly recognized by the Canadian court in its *Carter* decision: " 'Irremediable,'" the court said, "does not require the patient to undertake treatments that are not acceptable to the individual."[5] So what are we to say about a psychiatric patient who refuses all treatment for a mood or personality disorder and then requests PAD? The situation becomes particularly acute if there is reason to think that the treatment refusal stems from the disorder itself and that the patient might be less insistent on PAD were he or she to consent to treatment.

Perhaps once again some further precautions would be appropriate for these cases, such as an extended waiting period to determine whether the patient has a settled wish to die (this possibility is also discussed below). Of course, all of these difficulties can be avoided by imposing the terminal diagnosis requirement on all requests for PAD. But that, as we have seen, has its own problems.

What about people who are just "tired of life"?

Thus far we have been assuming that in order to qualify for PAD patients must have a medical condition (whether due to illness, accident, or disability) that is either terminal (Oregon) or serious and incurable (Belgium) or for which there is no prospect of improvement (the Netherlands). However, in the Netherlands there has been some pressure to expand the criteria to include persons who do not have a major illness that is either life-threatening or causing unbearable suffering but may instead have a constellation of more minor complaints that, in their eyes, combine to deprive their life of all further meaning. In 2010 a group called Out of Free Will collected over 100,000 signatures on a petition demanding that the Dutch Parliament amend the euthanasia law so that anyone over the age of seventy who feels "tired of life" should be able to request PAD. A number of prominent Dutch citizens supported the initiative, including former ministers and artists, legal scholars, and physicians.

Thus far the government has resisted this pressure. However, a survey conducted in 2015 showed that about a quarter of Dutch physicians could conceive of agreeing to PAD for patients with relatively minor medical complaints who were "tired of life" (this proportion declined to less than 20% if it was specified that the person in question had no medical condition causing suffering).[6] Furthermore, recent studies have shown that some requests for PAD on these grounds have been granted, both in the Netherlands and in Belgium.[7] It is easy to see how the logic of the Dutch case for legal PAD, which places much emphasis on the autonomy of the patient, could push the policy in this direction. If some octogenarian with a number of minor complaints decides that he or she has had enough, who is to question his or her judgment? If "existential suffering" can be a serious concern for patients who otherwise qualify for PAD on the grounds of a "grievous medical condition," why could it not be sufficient on its own?

On the other hand, it could be argued that since PAD is a form of medical treatment administered by physicians, it should be restricted to patients who present with serious medical conditions. Those who are simply fed up with living may seek such relief as they can find on their own, but they have no right to request the assistance of a medical practitioner to end their lives. Moreover, practitioners have the right to exercise professional judgment in determining whether a patient's request conforms to the stated criteria; they have no obligation to respond affirmatively to requests deemed to be groundless or frivolous. Or so the argument would go.

How do we determine decisional capacity?

Since we are dealing here with policies of voluntary PAD, we are presupposing patients who are decisionally capable both at the time the request is made and at the time the treatment is administered. The appropriate standard of decisional capacity is the one embedded in the doctrine of informed consent: the patient must have the ability to make reasoned decisions *about this kind of treatment*—that is, treatment that will hasten death. That capacity will include the patient's ability to understand his or her current diagnosis and prognosis, the available options for treating the condition (if any), the risks and benefits of each of these, the other available options for palliative treatment, and the implications of choosing an assisted death. Because of the finality of this choice, there is a case here for setting a high standard of decisional capacity. However, there seems no reason for it to be higher than the standard for other comparable end-of-life decisions, such as refusing life-sustaining treatment or requesting terminal sedation. The stakes are just as high for consent to these measures as for consent to PAD. For adults (eighteen years of age or over), decisional capacity should be the default presumption, which can be overturned only by evidence of impaired cognitive functioning.

Competency assessments—for both requests for and refusals of treatment—are already a familiar feature of end-of-life care. In that respect no new wrinkles are introduced by a practice of PAD. In the great majority of cases the attending physician will be able to determine with confidence whether the patient is decisionally capable. However, some cases will raise doubts, and in those cases referral to a competency specialist (psychologist or psychiatrist) may be indicated. Complications may be especially likely when patients present with psychiatric illnesses (either on their own or coupled with physical comorbidities). In these cases an additional level of scrutiny, beyond the judgment of the attending physician, may be called for.

Adults only?

The terms of the Oregon Death with Dignity Act restrict PAD to adults—that is, "individuals who are eighteen years of age or older." The same restriction holds in the other American states that have legalized PAD and in Colombia, Quebec, and Canada. However, as usual the Europeans do things differently. (Well, except for the Swiss, who allow PAD only for adults.) The Dutch law extends access to PAD beyond adults to "mature minors" between the ages of twelve and eighteen as long as they are "deemed to be capable of making a reasonable appraisal of their own interests" and their parents or guardians either have been consulted (ages sixteen to eighteen) or have consented (ages twelve to sixteen). The 2002 Belgian Law on Euthanasia required that patients requesting PAD be adults or "emancipated minors"—basically, persons under the age of eighteen who are independent of their parents (for example, due to marriage). It therefore did not apply to other "mature minors" (between the ages of twelve and eighteen). However, in 2014 the terms of the law were broadened to include "minors with the capacity of discernment" (that is, decisional capacity) who have a terminal diagnosis. In these cases the consent of the child's legal representatives is also required and a consultation with a child psychologist or psychiatrist is mandated. One could say therefore that Belgium currently has no minimum age for PAD. But it is probably more accurate to say that in Belgium eligibility for PAD is now determined by decisional capacity rather than by chronological age.

The case for including "mature minors" rests in part on the fact that in many jurisdictions they already have the right to refuse life-sustaining treatment. If an adolescent is competent to make that kind of life-and-death decision, then there seems no reason to deny the right to request PAD. In such cases it may be best to reverse the presumption of capacity so that adolescents will need to demonstrate that they have the maturity to handle a decision of this magnitude. If so, then the decision might be left in their hands, though consultation with parents or legal guardians may be mandated. Where minors lack the appropriate decisional capacity PAD can no longer be voluntary. Whether decisions can then be made for them by others is an issue we will consider later (in Chapter 9).

PAS or PAE?

As we know by now, PAD comes in two forms. So a policy of legal PAD must decide whether to include both and, if not, which is to be privileged. The legal regimes in the Benelux countries and in Canada are the most expansive, allowing access equally to PAS and physician-assisted euthanasia. Oregon and the other US states are more restrictive, confining access to PAS alone. Quebec and Colombia go the other way: PAE but not PAS.

We should be clear about the different protocols involved in the two forms of PAD. In the Netherlands PAE involves the injection by a physician of three separate drugs through an intravenous line: a sedative to relax the patient and induce sleep, a drug to put the patient into a coma and eliminate any reflexive movements, and a neuromuscular block to paralyze the muscles, including those involved in breathing. It is this third drug that causes death. The patient is attended by the physician throughout this process, which usually requires only minutes. By contrast, the protocol in Oregon calls for the physician to write a prescription, usually for secobarbital or pentobarbital, which the patient picks up at the pharmacy. The barbiturate is then mixed into a sweet drink such as juice. Because the barbiturate has a rather bitter taste, patients are usually instructed to take an antinausea medication beforehand to avoid regurgitating it. The patient then swallows the barbiturate at the time of his or her choosing. The physician is not present when this happens. The median time from ingestion to unconsciousness is about five minutes, and the time from ingestion to death is about half an hour.

. Once the step has been taken of legalizing PAD, the question is, Why would one want to discriminate between its two forms? As we have seen (Chapter 3), there is no ethical difference between them. The same considerations (of patient well-being and patient autonomy) that will justify the one will equally justify the other. Some commentators have stated a preference for PAS on the grounds that because the medication must be self-administered, the life-or-death decision is left in the patient's hands until the very end. But any decision in favor of PAE is revocable at any time, and doctors will routinely ask their patients whether they wish to change their minds before taking the final step of administering the medication. There seems no meaningful practical difference here.

Indeed, the ethical verdict would appear to go the other way. PAS is available only to patients who are physically capable of orally ingesting the medication. But some patients who would otherwise qualify for PAD do not have this capacity, either because they lack the use of their hands (through upper-body paralysis) or because they are unable to swallow (as in the late stages of ALS). It therefore appears discriminatory to offer only PAS and not PAE as well. Administration of the medication through an intravenous line is also more efficient and faster-acting than oral administration; for one thing, there is no risk of the patient regurgitating the drugs (which has been known to happen in Oregon). This may partially explain why, in the Benelux countries where both forms of PAD are available, about 90% of patients prefer PAE to PAS.

In Oregon and the other US states the difference between the two forms of PAD appears to be political rather than ethical. The ballot initiative that eventually led to legalization in Oregon was first put to voters in 1994. Ballot initiatives to legalize both PAS and PAE had recently failed in two neighboring states: Washington in 1991 and California in 1992. Opinion polls tended to show that Americans were less averse to PAS than to PAE. The decision was therefore made in Oregon to seek voter approval for legalization of PAS alone. Once that initiative succeeded, Oregon became the template for ballot initiatives in Washington and Colorado and for legislative initiatives in Vermont and California. Once a winning formula has been found, it only makes sense to stick with it. There has been no movement in Oregon to broaden the policy to include PAE, and initiatives in other states will inevitably continue to press the Oregon model.

What procedures should be required?

PAD is a treatment request, not a treatment refusal. A patient can refuse life-sustaining treatment simply by saying "no" to it or by declining to sign a consent form. It is standard for regulatory policies concerning PAD to require that requests be in writing and that they be properly witnessed. The patient's written request then becomes part of the documentary record of the treatment. In the event that a patient is physically incapable of signing a written document, some other legally recognized means of registering the request can be provided. A requirement that the request be repeated at least once over a period of, say, a few days may also be appropriate in order to determine that this decision represents the patient's settled frame of mind. However, this requirement should be flexible to accommodate cases in which the patient's suffering would make it an act of cruelty to enforce a delay. On the other hand, for some nonterminal illnesses, especially psychiatric conditions or traumatic injury, it might make sense to require patients to reaffirm their decision over a longer period of time. Whatever the time frame, a request must be revocable by the patient at any time.

Whatever form the patient's request takes, it must be both voluntary and informed. In order to be voluntary, it must be free of undue influence, whether by family, friends, or health care providers. Influence will be "undue" when it rises to the level of fraud, deceit, duress, or coercion. A patient's decision should be deemed to be voluntary unless there is some reason to think that it is not, in which case the patient should be offered counseling or access to a trusted adviser. In order for the request to be informed, the patient must be provided with adequate information concerning the diagnosis and prognosis, the treatment options (both therapeutic and palliative) that are available, the probable outcome of each of these options, and the risks attached to each option. In short, he or she must be given all the information that a reasonable person in the same circumstances would require in order to make a reasoned decision to hasten death (whether by PAD or any other end-of-life measure). In order to ensure that the patient is adequately informed about other palliative treatment options, it may be sound practice to offer a consultation with a palliative care team.

So far, the decision whether to proceed with PAD is a matter between a patient and his or her physician. However, as a safeguard most jurisdictions require consultation with a second physician who is not part of the patient's care team. The consulting physician must decide whether to confirm the attending physician's diagnosis of the patient's condition and the eligibility of the patient for PAD under the criteria in the prevailing policy. We should keep in mind that neither a patient's attending physician nor the consulting physician is obliged to grant a request for PAD (in the Benelux countries about a third of requests are refused). In the case of refusal by either physician, the patient is, of course, entitled to seek a further opinion.

As mentioned earlier, patients presenting with psychiatric illnesses may pose special problems. If the attending physician is in doubt about the patient's decisional capacity, then referral for a competency assessment may be in order. If the issue is whether or not the patient's condition qualifies as "incurable" or "irremediable," then a further consult with a psychiatrist may be indicated. Whatever form it takes, a somewhat stricter level of scrutiny for cases in this category may be appropriate. If patients with psychiatric illnesses can qualify for PAD at all under the terms of a policy (as we saw earlier, in some jurisdictions they cannot), they will constitute only a small fraction of the overall caseload. But the experience of the Benelux countries shows that they are likely to be among the most difficult and controversial cases.

In the next section we will consider the sort of subsequent review to which cases of PAD should be subject. However, some commentators have responded to the difficulties likely to be posed by some psychiatric cases by proposing a system of prior review. Under this scheme the decision whether to proceed with PAD would no longer be made just by a patient and his or her attending physician (together with the consulting physician) but would also require prior approval by an authoritative tribunal or even a court. The system can be proposed either just for hard cases (such as some psychiatric patients) or for all cases. The latter proposal seems a disproportionate response to the problem. The experience of the Benelux jurisdictions shows that 97%–99% of all patients will present with serious physical illnesses, nearly all of which will be easy cases. Furthermore, not all cases of psychiatric illness will be hard ones; some will concern patients who have suffered from severe and treatment-resistant symptoms for years. So a blanket requirement of prior review will impose on all patients a further time-consuming bureaucratic process that is needed only for the less than 1% of cases that are difficult. For patients with end-stage cancer, who will comprise about 80% of requests for PAD, a further delay of even days can be agonizing. For the small minority of hard cases, however, such review may indeed be appropriate as a further safeguard. Alternatively, referral of the cases to a consultative body without decision-making authority may provide the additional resource that doctors need.

What system of review and oversight would be appropriate?

Virtually every system of legal PAD agrees on the importance of transparency and effective regulation. In the service of these aims all cases of PAD must be fully documented at every stage in the process and reported as such to an appropriate oversight body. This body has two potential tasks: to review individual cases in order to ensure compliance with both substantive criteria and procedural regulations and to collect data and issue periodic reports on the operation of the policy.

In Oregon the latter function is performed by the state Public Health Division, which compiles anonymized statistics and publishes annual reports. However, it does not conduct a case-by-case review. In the Netherlands both tasks are handled by the five Regional Review Committees, which have the authority to flag deviations from the prescribed rules and to refer cases to the public prosecutor. The five committees issue a combined annual report with data summarizing all cases reported to them. The same dual functions are performed in Belgium by the Federal Control and Evaluation Commission. In Quebec the law that determined the criteria and procedures for legal PAD also set up an End of Life Commission tasked both with ensuring compliance and with reporting on the operation of the law. In a federal system like that of Canada the review and reporting functions may be somewhat detached since the regulation of medical services falls under provincial jurisdiction, while data collection should ideally cover the country as a whole.

What should be done about conscientious objection?

Assisted death is a controversial matter. Some physicians will have no religious or ethical objection to providing this service for their patients, while for others it will violate the dictates of their conscience. Policies typically include a "conscience clause" that enables providers to decline to offer the service on grounds of personal conviction. However, the conscience rights of physicians must be balanced against the access rights of their patients. Doctors are obliged not to abandon patients who request PAD. Instead, they must be willing to take whatever steps are necessary to ensure that the patient has effective access to the service. What this may require of them will vary from case to case, from providing information on how the patient can access the service to referral and transfer of care to a willing provider.

Likewise, some health care institutions will be unwilling to allow PAD on their premises if it is inconsistent with their mission statement. Where these institutions are publicly funded a decision must be made as to whether to allow them to opt out, especially since some physicians attached to the institution may themselves be willing providers.

7

WHAT IS THE CASE IN FAVOR
OF LEGALIZATION?

What is the relationship between ethics and law?

Earlier we discussed the ethical status of physician-assisted death, surveying (in Chapters 3 and 4) arguments for and against its justifiability. There the focus was on what it might be right or wrong for particular agents to do on particular occasions: for instance, whether it would be wrong for a doctor to provide PAD for a competent patient who requests it while experiencing intolerable suffering from a serious and untreatable illness. Now we move on to consider normative questions at a different level: not what individual doctors (or patients) should do but what the law regarding PAD should be.

It is tempting to think that your answer to this legal question should be determined by your answer to the earlier ethical question. But this would be a mistake. The ethical status of practices of PAD is neither necessary nor sufficient to determine their legal status. For one thing, when we shift from the ethical question to the legal a host of additional factors come into play because we are now debating not just the outcome of a particular act but the impact on society at large of a broad public policy. These factors will include the enforceability of a policy, the costs of its enforcement, the burden of its sanctions, and its spillover effects on third parties.

It is not inconsistent to think that some practice is morally wrong but should nonetheless be legally permitted. Commonplace instances concern small-scale wrongs, such as everyday lies or broken promises, which are just too trivial to be any concern of the law. But there are more serious examples as well. Adultery, for example, can do devastating harm to the deceived spouse, but it might be quite inappropriate, indeed counterproductive, to criminalize this behavior (as opposed to recognizing it as valid grounds for divorce). Some people who think abortion wrong do not support a criminal ban on the procedure, on the grounds that it would likely drive women to seek much-riskier illegal abortions.

It is also not inconsistent to think that some practice is morally permissible but should not be legally permitted. Again this could be due to factors that are legally, but not ethically, salient. Perhaps no law can be crafted that would allow just the narrow set of morally permissible cases while excluding the impermissible ones. Perhaps there are strong pragmatic reasons to hold the line here, the cost of prohibiting some morally acceptable cases being necessary in order to prevent morally unacceptable ones. Many reasonable people take this view about PAD. They concede that there are instances in which assisting a suicide or administering euthanasia can be the right thing to do, but they do not trust the ability of any legal policy to discriminate these cases from the others in which it is wrong. Or they think that a policy that allows any PAD will inevitably impose unacceptable risks on vulnerable third parties. They therefore believe that some ethically permissible practices should be legally impermissible.

Thus, in this book I separate the ethical question from the legal one. One need not take the view that they are entirely independent of one another. Some of the factors relevant to settling the ethical status of PAD will no doubt also be relevant to determining its legal status. But even if we manage to arrive at a set of ethical conclusions about PAD with which we are perfectly comfortable, there will still be further issues to be resolved before deciding on a legal policy. It is to those issues that we now turn by first considering the arguments in favor of a policy of legal PAD. In the last chapter we saw just how many different kinds of policy are possible. The pro arguments will apply equally to any policy within the very broad range of available options. When we come to examine the con arguments in the next chapter, we may need to be more specific about the kind of policy in question.

What is the argument from compassion?

The case for a policy of legal PAD rests in part on the same two values that pervaded our earlier ethical discussion: well-being and autonomy. But because we are now talking about issues of public policy, it is appropriate to formulate the appeal to these values in somewhat different terms. One of the civic virtues we expect of citizens in any decent society is compassion. We may take compassion to include both sympathy for those who find themselves in terrible circumstances and a disposition to do what we can to help them. Compassion is owed to those whose lives have been blighted by natural disaster, war, poverty, bigotry, abuse, or personal violence. It is at least partly on the basis of compassion that decent societies send aid to victims of natural disasters and welcome refugees who are fleeing war zones or systemic persecution on the basis of their gender or sexuality or political opinions. But compassion, it will be argued, is also owed to those in the dying process, if that process is accompanied by serious suffering.

It is for these people that hospice palliative care was developed as a means of making the end of life as comfortable as possible. We have already canvassed some of the resources that can be marshaled to deal with suffering, whether it is physical or psychosocial. But experience shows that even the best palliative care may be unable to alleviate all sources of suffering.[1] The most dramatic form of suffering, and the one for whose management palliative medicine has the most effective means at its disposal, is physical pain. Modern pharmacology can provide adequate pain relief for most patients in the end-stages of debilitating illnesses such as cancer. Most patients, but not all.[2] Other symptoms—nausea, vomiting, dizziness, agitation, delirium, shortness of breath, severe itching, pressure sores, offensive odors from wounds—are typically harder to alleviate than pain. Furthermore, for many people these strictly physical symptoms, distressing though they might be, are not their only—or even their most important—concern in the dying process. Patients who have sought an assisted suicide in Oregon, where it is legally available, tend to cite other motivating factors as more significant, including loss of independence or control, indignity, loss of a sense of self, and diminished ability to engage in the activities that made their lives meaningful.[3] Most of these patients are already in hospice when they request an assisted suicide, and their strictly physical symptoms are under adequate control. Their suffering is instead psychosocial, consisting in the conviction that their illness has robbed their life of all point or meaning. Similarly, a study of requests for euthanasia over a twenty-five-year period in the Netherlands found that pain had declined dramatically as a motivating reason, paralleled by an increase in the importance of such factors as hopelessness and deteriorating health.[4]

For these forms of suffering palliative medicine may have little to offer. There is, of course, more to good-quality palliative care than the administration of drugs. But even such nonpharmacological resources as counseling or companionship may fail to restore meaning to life. In short, just as we have the concept of medical futility for cases in which any further treatment of the patient's disease condition would be useless, so we must also face the fact of palliative futility, when none of the standard palliative measures can restore to the patient a life worth living.

As we have already seen, patients in these dire circumstances have various means available to them of escaping further suffering by hastening their death. They can, of course, refuse all further treatment of their disease condition. If they are in palliative care, then they will probably have already done this, but they can still refuse food and fluids and elect to die of dehydration. If they are suffering intractable physical symptoms, then they can request terminal sedation. For many patients in the dying process one or another of these measures may suffice. But the experience of jurisdictions in which assisted death is legal shows that some patients—not many—will prefer it to these other options. Indeed, even where it is not legal many patients at the end of life express a strong interest in assisted death.[5]

We may think of the big picture in the following way. In developed societies a majority of people die in health care institutions rather than at home. For a majority of these people some end-of-life treatment decisions are made. A minority of this majority, mainly those with advanced cancers, will decide to forgo any further treatment of their disease condition and enter palliative care. A minority of that minority will continue to find their symptoms (whether physical or psychosocial) sufficiently distressing that they will wish to hasten their death. Some members of this group will want to achieve this end by means of PAD (rather than, say, refusal of food and fluids). Their numbers will not be great (no more than 3% of all annual deaths in a given jurisdiction), but their suffering will. It is the mark of a compassionate society that it respond most to those minorities whose need is greatest. Most legal jurisdictions still permit patients access to all palliative measures with the exception of PAD. In drawing this legal bright line these regimes deny some patients—including many whose present condition and future prospects are the grimmest—access to what they themselves believe to be the best remedy for their suffering. In doing this they fail the test of compassion.

What is the argument from respect?

They also fail the test of respect. The basis of respect for others is a willingness to acknowledge their right to make their own decisions about their lives in accordance with their own value system. In other words, respect is directed at autonomy or self-determination, just as compassion is directed at suffering or hardship. A society that practices the civic virtue of respect makes allowance for diversity and difference and understands that the customs and lifestyles of others may be just as meaningful for them as ours are for us, though they may seem strange or even incomprehensible to us. If respect requires allowing others to live their lives according to their own lights, then it must also allow them to manage their dying process in the same way.

In medical contexts respect foregrounds choice, consent, request, refusal. It allows patients to choose for themselves which of the array of end-of-life measures will best enable them to manage the dying process on their own terms. No one size here fits all; people just differ in the importance they attach to certain life conditions (independence, say, or control) and in what they take to be their cultural or spiritual commitments. For the minority who will choose PAD when presented with the option, their choice is an affirmation of their values, their priorities, and their self-determination. Any jurisdiction that denies them this option treats them with disrespect.

What is the argument from freedom of conscience?

Both of the preceding arguments for the legalization of PAD closely parallel the arguments for its ethical acceptability since they appeal to the same basic values of well-being and autonomy. They may therefore support the idea that the legal status of PAD depends on its ethical status. There is, however, a further argument that entirely separates the two questions. To see how it goes it may be helpful to turn attention away from PAD for a moment to another issue with which it has some affinities: abortion.

Most people's view about the morality of abortion turns on their view of the moral status of a fetus: whether it has anything like the same rights as a developed, adult person. As anyone who has dipped into the massive literature on this issue can attest, the arguments on both sides can get pretty complex and sophisticated. Even with the best will it can be very difficult to determine which side of the debate has the better case. One way of responding to this fact is to say that this is an issue on which reasonable people can disagree. After thinking through the issue, you may be pretty sure you've got the right answer, but you must recognize that other people—seemingly just as reasonable as you—are equally convinced by the contrary answer. This recognition of the fact of reasonable disagreement will be reinforced if, for example, public opinion polls on the subject show a deep split in people's convictions.

In light of this fact, what is the appropriate public policy concerning abortion? Should women be permitted to seek abortions or not? One deep-seated principle underlying liberal societies—and often embedded in their constitutionally guaranteed rights—is freedom of conscience.

Its basic idea is that when an ethical issue is unsettled or deeply divisive—that is, when it is subject to reasonable disagreement—the state must not impose the views of one party to the debate on those who disagree with them. These are matters on which everyone must be free to decide on the basis of his or her own conscience. A policy of allowing women to decide for themselves whether to seek an abortion violates no one's freedom of conscience, for it does not compel anyone to have an abortion, or to provide one, against his or her will. But the same cannot be said for a policy that prohibits abortion since it violates the freedom of conscience of women who have no moral objection to it and would seek it if they could. The only defensible societal response therefore to the fact of reasonable disagreement over the moral status of abortion is laissez-faire. Some people who believe that abortion is wrong— because it violates a fetus's right to life—defend this policy position because they recognize that other equally reasonable people disagree on this point and, in light of this recognition, accept that it would be improper for the law to enforce their particular moral view. They regard abortion as morally impermissible but think that it should be legally permitted.

This was the very position articulated by former New York State governor Mario Cuomo in September 1984 in a speech he delivered to the Department of Theology at the University of Notre Dame.[6] Cuomo was a devout Catholic and fully accepted his church's teaching on abortion: "As Catholics, my wife and I were enjoined never to use abortion to destroy the life we created, and we never have. We thought Church doctrine was clear on this, and— more than that—both of us felt it in full agreement with what our hearts and our consciences told us. For me life or fetal life in the womb should be protected." However, Cuomo also drew a vital distinction between his private beliefs as a Catholic and his public responsibilities as governor of a diverse, secular state:

> The Catholic who holds political office in a pluralistic democracy—who is elected to serve Jews and Moslems, atheists and Protestants, as well as Catholics—bears special responsibility. He or she undertakes to help create conditions under which all can live with a maximum of dignity and with a reasonable degree of freedom; where everyone who chooses may hold beliefs different from specifically Catholic ones—sometimes contradictory to them; where the laws protect people's right to divorce, to use birth control, and even to choose abortion.

Cuomo therefore concluded that, as a politician, he could not support a constitutional amendment banning abortion or the denial of public funding to impoverished women who sought abortions in his state. Cuomo was, of course, addressing the specific interplay between his religiously based ethical beliefs, on the one hand, and the formation of public policy, on the other. But nothing changes if the beliefs are not faith-based. Religious doctrines are simply the paradigmatic sites of reasonable disagreement, where everyone must make up his or her own mind about what to believe and none can be branded unreasonable simply for dissenting. What Cuomo saw, where abortion is concerned, was that no belief, however strongly held, can be imposed on those who disagree with it unless it is possible to show that their disagreement is arbitrary or unreasonable.

The extrapolation of this lesson to the case of PAD is straightforward. It should be obvious from the earlier chapters that the ethical issues concerning PAD are complex and intricate. It is to be expected that reasonable people will come to contrary conclusions about them. In that case the only political resolution that equally respects the conscience rights of all is a policy that allows access to PAD for those who need it and have no ethical objection to it. While one's own conscience might firmly reject any form of assisted death, it should also require the law to respect the consciences of those who disagree.

This argument in favor of legalization is potentially very powerful since it starts with only a very weak premise. It does not require agreeing that well-being and autonomy are basic values for bioethics or that compassion and respect are the corresponding civic virtues. It only requires acknowledging that the ethical status of PAD is a contested issue on which reasonable persons may come to contrary conclusions. Wherever you stand on the ethical issue, that much seems obvious.

What is the argument from parity?

It is a fundamental principle of equity that the law should treat like cases alike (and different cases differently). Where criminal law is concerned, this principle would imply that if one practice is legally permitted while another is prohibited, then there had better be some relevant difference between them. You often hear this principle invoked in arguments about the legalization of drugs like cannabis. Tobacco and alcohol are legal substances, the argument goes, and cannabis is less harmful than either of them, so equity dictates that it should be legal as well.

In most legal jurisdictions—except those that have legalized PAD—the law distinguishes between PAD and other end-of-life treatment options that may also hasten death, including refusal of life-sustaining treatment, pain management through high doses of opioids, and terminal sedation. This distinction is justifiable only if there is some relevant difference between PAD and these other options. As we have seen (Chapter 4), many people believe that there is an ethical "bright line" between PAD and these other measures such that the latter are all ethically permissible (under conditions of patient choice and patient best interest) while the former is ethically impermissible (under the same conditions). However, as we have also seen, it is very difficult to establish the basis for this "bright line," whether the appeal is to the right to life, the sanctity of life, the doctrine of double effect, or the doctrine of doing and allowing. If all of these efforts fail, then there may be no significant ethical difference between PAD and these other treatment modalities. But in that case the legal distinction between them is arbitrary and unjustified; if these other measures are legal, then PAD should be legal as well.

However, as so stated, this argument is incomplete in at least two different ways. First, it seeks parity of legal status for all end-of-life treatment options that may have the effect of hastening death. However, there are two different ways in which this parity could be achieved: either permit them all or prohibit them all. It is therefore open to the opponent of legalization to respond by accepting that all measures that might hasten death should be unlawful.

This is likely to be too big a bullet for opponents to bite since, as we have seen (Chapter 5), the legality of patient refusal of treatment, administration of potent painkillers, and terminal sedation is pretty firmly entrenched. So we turn to the second source of incompleteness in the argument from parity. As stated so far, it contains the assumption that the only legally relevant difference between PAD and the legally permitted end-of-life treatments must be an ethical one. If they are ethically equivalent, the argument goes, then they must also be legally equivalent. But this need not be so. They could also differ in another relevant respect that is not ethical but practical. Opponents of legalization often argue that PAD cannot be legalized safely without putting vulnerable persons at risk, either because any safeguards that are put in place will be open to abuse or because a "slippery slope" will eventually lead to ethically unacceptable practices. If these contentions can be supported and if no similar dangers accompany the legalization of the other end-of-life treatments, then this could constitute a relevant difference that would justify a legal ban on PAD but not on these other measures. Whether the contentions can be supported is a question we will explore in the next chapter. Until those issues are resolved, therefore, the argument from parity will remain inconclusive.

What is the argument from democracy?

The idea of legalizing some form of PAD has been on the public agenda in the United States, with varying degrees of prominence, since at least the 1990s. For any informed member of the public, therefore, it is not exactly a novel idea. In recognition of this fact the topic has long been a regular item in public opinion surveys, including the Gallup organization's annual Values and Beliefs Survey. The most recent result of that survey (conducted in May 2015) showed that 68% of respondents favored legalizing physician-assisted suicide.[7]

Poll results on this issue often need to be interpreted with some care since responses are known to be sensitive to the phrasing of the question. In particular, it has sometimes seemed to matter whether the question includes the term *suicide*, with its often-pejorative connotations. However, it is noteworthy that the Gallup survey did include the "s" word. Here is the question put to respondents: "When a person has a disease that cannot be cured and is living in severe pain, do you think doctors should or should not be allowed by law to assist the patient to commit suicide if the patient requests it?" Besides the explicit mention of physician-assisted suicide, this question included three of the conditions standardly imposed on its legalization: (1) an incurable illness, (2) serious suffering, and (3) a voluntary request by the patient. (Interestingly, it did not include the stipulation that the illness be terminal.) This was the question to which 68% said doctors should be so allowed and 28% said that they should not. Over the years the same question has always elicited a majority in favor of legal PAS, ranging from a low of 52% in 1997 to a high of 68% in 2001 and 2015.

Gallup did find that the level of support for legalization tended to be significantly higher when the question was formulated without the "s" word. They also asked respondents a second question: "When a person has a disease that cannot be cured, do you think doctors should be allowed by law to end the patient's life by some painless means if the patient and his or her family request it?" In the 2015 survey 70% of respondents gave affirmative answers to this question, a result virtually identical to the PAS formulation. But over the years the level of affirmative responses to this question has tended to be much higher than to the PAS question, varying from a low of 68% in 2001 to a high of 75% in 2005. This is despite the fact that in the second question there is no reference to the patient's suffering, just to the incurability of the disease, and the fact that the doctor's role here would most readily be interpreted as physician-assisted euthanasia rather than PAS.

While it is worth noting the dependence of these poll results on the precise formulation of the question, it is also easy to make too much of it. The fact is that every question that Gallup has posed on legalizing PAD has elicited a majority in support for nearly twenty years, regardless of how it has been phrased. It seems safe to conclude, therefore, that a strong majority of Americans endorse the legalization of PAD in some form and under some set of conditions. Further evidence for this hypothesis is provided by the success of the ballot initiatives in Oregon (1994 and 1997), Washington (2008), and Colorado (2016), each of which returned a majority in favor of legalizing PAS. These referendum results also serve to show that opinions need not waver when the context of decision is real rather than merely hypothetical and when people have been exposed to arguments on both sides of the question. (However, a similar ballot initiative in Massachusetts, based very closely on the Oregon PAS policy, narrowly failed in 2012, though antecedently there did appear to be a majority in favor of it.)

In its simplest form the argument from democracy would go somewhat as follows: (1) in a democracy the will of a majority of the people should prevail; (2) a majority of Americans favor legalizing PAD; therefore (3) PAD should be legal in the United States. As noted in the previous chapter, the legislatures of two states (Vermont and California) have legalized PAS without benefit of a prior referendum. But similar bills have been defeated in many other state legislatures, often by very substantial margins. It is this disconnect between public opinion and legislative inaction that the argument from democracy challenges.

As stated, the argument is in need of some pretty obvious qualifications. For one thing, the opinion survey results measure the views of Americans nationally, while the legal status of PAD is a matter to be settled by the states. So the most that could be claimed is that state legislatures should legalize PAD if there is majority support for this result in their own state. Having said that, it seems pretty obvious that there must be many states in which this support exists.

The argument also makes some controversial assumptions about the role of legislators—namely, that their votes should always reflect the majority will among their constituents. This is certainly not the only view on this matter. Others might argue that legislators are elected to exercise their own judgment on matters of public policy and that this is what they should do when the PAD issue comes up, even if their judgment flies in the face of public opinion. This is not the place to resolve this dispute in political science. Whatever the proper role of an elected legislator, it can still be argued to be a defect in the democratic process if the collective judgment of a legislative body on an issue like PAD departs so strikingly from public opinion.

Finally, the argument from democracy also needs a quite different qualification. If we think that legislatures should enact policies favored by the majority, that must be on the condition that what the majority favors is not patently unjust or otherwise morally unconscionable. Majorities, after all, can support evil as well as good. A majority of citizens in the southern states supported slavery prior to the Civil War (and probably for some time thereafter), a majority of Germans in the 1930s supported the Nazis' military ambitions and their persecution of the Jews, and a majority of Americans in the early 1940s supported the internment of Japanese citizens and residents, but in none of these cases do we want to say that the policy in question gained legitimacy from that level of popular support. The most we could say, therefore, on behalf of the argument from democracy is that legislative action should mirror public opinion when that opinion is independently morally defensible. Whether PAD is morally defensible is the issue we explored in Chapters 3 and 4. The strength of the argument from democracy therefore depends in part on how that issue is resolved.

8

WHAT IS THE CASE AGAINST?

What is the slippery slope argument?

As the arguments in the previous chapter show, a strong case can be made for legalizing physician-assisted death. However, this is far from the end of the matter. While some opponents of legalization object to it on ethical grounds— usually by invoking some version of the sanctity of life— the most important and influential objections are, at least on the face of them, not ethical but practical. All of these objections take the same basic form: they concede that a regime providing legal access to PAD would benefit some dying patients, but they contend that it would come at too high a cost to others. This line of response to the case for legalization raises issues of public risk that were not on the table in our ethical discussion. Articulating and assessing them is the business of this chapter.

The practical objections to a regulatory policy for PAD rest on claims of fact and must therefore be supported by evidence. Public policy—on any issue, but certainly on this one—must be evidence-based. Physician-assisted suicide has been legal in Oregon since 1997, and both forms of PAD have been fully legal in the Netherlands and Belgium since 2002. There is an enormous amount of empirical evidence on how the policies in these jurisdictions have worked out in practice. There is no excuse for not consulting and utilizing this information. To paraphrase the *X-Files*, the facts are out there; all we need to do is look for them.

In an often-cited article published nearly sixty years ago a legal scholar named Yale Kamisar established the gold standard for objections to legalized PAD. Kamisar observed, correctly, that proponents of legalization often assumed that arguments on the other side of the question were necessarily religious in character. To counteract this assumption he set out to formulate what he considered to be the main nonreligious objections. After acknowledging that an ethical case could be made for PAD, at least in some circumstances, he summarized those objections in the following way: "I see the issue, then, as the need for voluntary euthanasia versus (1) the incidence of mistake and abuse; and (2) the danger that legal machinery initially designed to kill those who are a nuisance to themselves may someday engulf those who are a nuisance to others."[1] These two objections to legalization remain the most frequently heard in the present day.

It is important to distinguish them, as Kamisar did, for they are quite different. The difference can be best illustrated if we assume a particular kind of legal policy as our baseline. In Chapter 6 we noted the various forms that a policy of legal PAD can take, from more restrictive to more expansive. For the present purposes it will be convenient to assume a fairly restrictive policy, such as the one in place in Oregon, which has since served as the model for legislation in Washington, Vermont, California, and Colorado. Under the terms of the Oregon policy, you will recall, PAS is permitted but not physician-assisted euthanasia, and patients must be diagnosed with a terminal illness (that is, have a life expectancy of less than six months). Kamisar's first objection rests on the claim that the various conditions built into a policy of this sort will inevitably be violated, either unintentionally (mistake) or intentionally (abuse), so that cases of PAD will occur that are not authorized by the terms of the policy. This is the *abuse argument*. His second objection rests on the claim that those conditions will inevitably be expanded so that cases of PAD that are not now authorized by the terms of the Oregon policy will come in time to be authorized by an expanded policy. This is the *slippery slope argument*.

The common feature of the two arguments is the claim that while the cases of PAD permitted by the terms of the policy as written may be ethically justified, implementing the policy will inevitably lead to cases that are unjustified. The arguments differ in the way in which they envisage this slippage from the justified to the unjustified occurring: the former argument claims that it will occur even if the terms of the policy remain unchanged, while the latter argument attributes it to a change in those terms. (While the arguments are different, they are obviously quite compatible with one another; Kamisar employs both, as do many other critics.)

Of the two arguments, the latter is the easier to deal with. It will be the subject of this section, with the issues around mistake and abuse addressed in the next. As we are envisaging it, the slippery slope argument consists of two claims, both of which must be true for the argument to have any force:

> *The empirical claim.* If the Oregon policy is implemented, then (certainly, inevitably, or at least highly probably) it will mutate into an expanded policy.
>
> *The normative claim.* At least some cases of assisted death permitted by the expanded policy (but not by the Oregon policy) will be ethically unacceptable.

The problem for the argument is that it is difficult to find (or imagine) an expanded policy such that both claims are true. It is easy to make the normative claim true by invoking what Kamisar calls the "parade of horrors": the Nazi death camps or the "euthanasia program" aimed at eliminating the "mentally deficient" and otherwise "unfit." But these examples of what might lie at the bottom of the ethical slope spectacularly fail to satisfy the empirical claim. No sane person thinks that the Oregon policy is going to lead to genocide or that this would be the outcome if the policy were implemented in any other jurisdiction.

In a more recent article Kamisar has suggested that it will be impossible for a narrow policy like Oregon's to hold two lines: between PAS and PAE and between terminal and nonterminal cases.[2] These empirical claims are much more plausible. As it happens, there has been little interest to date in Oregon, or in any of the other states that have adopted the Oregon model, in either of these expansions. But we have the example of the Benelux countries in which both lines have been crossed: both PAS and PAE are permitted, and there is no requirement of a terminal condition (since the policies there focus on suffering rather than life expectancy). So let us assume that a future expansion of the Oregon policy in either or both of these directions is at least possible. The problem is that neither expansion seems to lead to practices that are ethically unacceptable. As we saw in Chapter 3, there is no significant ethical difference between PAS and PAE. Indeed, there is a case to be made that a policy that permits PAE as well as PAS is more humane since it will include patients whose physical illness or disability prevents them from self-administering life-ending medication (if, for instance, they are paralyzed or unable to swallow). The same can be said for a policy that drops the restriction to terminal illnesses (in the Oregon sense) since it will permit PAE for patients with conditions such as quadriplegia or locked-in syndrome that are not themselves terminal but nonetheless have a severe impact on quality of life. It can also be argued that a focus on patient suffering rather than patient longevity is ethically preferable since the primary purpose of end-of-life palliative care should be to reduce or eliminate suffering.

So far we don't have an example of an expanded Oregon policy that satisfies both the empirical and the normative claims: where the former is satisfied, the latter is not and vice versa. However, there are other possibilities. One is that if the criteria shift from requiring a terminal illness to requiring an illness that causes intolerable suffering, then the scope of the concept of suffering will itself expand so as to include psychological as well as strictly physical symptoms. But this has already occurred in Oregon, where the main reasons cited by patients for requesting PAS are psychological or "existential" in nature. Alternatively, dropping the terminal illness requirement might lead to the inclusion of mental as well as physical illnesses as qualifiers for PAD. As we have seen, this has already happened in the Benelux countries. The inclusion of psychiatric illnesses can certainly cause further complications for a policy—complications that we surveyed in Chapter 6. But if such illnesses can at least sometimes satisfy the eligibility criteria, by being "serious" and "incurable" and causing "intolerable suffering," then it does not seem ethically unacceptable for a policy to include them. Indeed, it can be argued that it would be indefensible to exclude them.

Things get a little trickier if we imagine the eligibility criteria weakened enough to include people whose suffering is wholly "existential" and who are just "tired of life." No extant policy has yet been formally amended so as to include such cases. Although there has been pressure in the Netherlands to expand the current policy in this direction, the Dutch government has so far resisted it. However, recent studies have shown that some assisted deaths are already occurring on this ground in both the Netherlands and Belgium.[3] Furthermore, a recent survey of Dutch physicians found that about a quarter of them could conceive of granting a request for PAD from a person who was "tired of life."[4] So let us concede that an expansion in this direction is at least possible, or even probable, thereby satisfying the empirical claim. What about the normative claim? Is providing PAD for elderly patients who do not have a "serious" illness but are "tired of life" ethically unacceptable? The issue seems to me debatable, with no clear resolution either way. Providing PAD for such patients seems unlikely to qualify as the kind of moral horror that lies at the bottom of the slippery slope.

The same conclusion seems appropriate for another possible expansion: from a policy of "adults only" to the inclusion of at least some children. Once again Oregon has held the line here, as have the other American states that have adopted the Oregon model. But, as we have seen, the Dutch law has included "mature minors" since its adoption in 2002, and the Belgian policy has recently been amended so that eligibility for PAD is now based on decisional capacity rather than age. A strong ethical case can be made that patients who otherwise qualify for PAD, on grounds of a "serious" and "incurable" illness and "intolerable suffering," should not be excluded simply on grounds of chronological age. Some will undoubtedly disagree, but that just makes the question debatable. Once again, no moral horror here.

However, one further possible expansion remains to be considered: from voluntary to nonvoluntary PAD. So far we have confined ourselves to voluntary requests for PAD from patients who are decisionally capable at both the time of the request and the time of the resulting procedure. But there will be cases in which capacity is lost as a result of conditions such as dementia or permanent unconsciousness. Is it likely that a policy of voluntary PAD will expand in this direction? And if it did, would this expansion be ethically unacceptable? These questions we will postpone to the next chapter.

Leaving that issue aside, it is difficult to think of any expansion of an Oregon-like policy that is empirically likely (let alone certain) and that would result in permitting patently unacceptable cases of PAD. The policy therefore does not seem readily susceptible to slippery slope objections. Before leaving the topic, however, it is worth pointing out that if you want to run a slippery slope argument for end-of-life measures, then the practice at the top of the slope is not assisted suicide or euthanasia but refusal of life-sustaining treatment. What is ethically problematic about all of the end-of-life measures we have surveyed is their capacity to hasten death. Once we have accepted any of them—even treatment refusal—we have accepted that hastening death is ethically permissible and we are on the top of the slope. From that vantage point the administration of high-dose opioids, terminal sedation, assisted suicide, voluntary euthanasia, and nonvoluntary euthanasia are just further points on the slope. If you want to stay off the slope entirely, then you must reject most of the currently available end-of-life treatment measures.

What is the abuse argument?

Of all the practical arguments against the legalization of PAD, concerns about mistake or abuse stand out as the most common and the most influential. When courts have refused to overrule laws governing assisted death, they have done so primarily on the ground that a blanket prohibition is necessary in order to protect vulnerable sectors of the population. This was the principal ground of Justice Sopinka's opinion, writing for the majority of the Canadian

Supreme Court in the 1993 *Rodriguez* case: "In order to effectively protect life and those who are vulnerable in society, a prohibition without exception on the giving of assistance to commit suicide is the best approach."[5] Likewise Chief Justice Rehnquist for the US Supreme Court in its 1997 *Glucksberg* decision:

> The constitutional requirement that Washington's assisted suicide ban be rationally related to legitimate government interests ... is unquestionably met here. These interests include ... protecting the poor, the elderly, disabled persons, the terminally ill, and persons in other vulnerable groups from indifference, prejudice, and psychological and financial pressure to end their lives.[6]

The issue of protecting the vulnerable has also been uppermost in the minds of critics of legalization from Kamisar onward. The first step in dealing with it is to distinguish the two aspects of the issue—mistake and abuse—that Kamisar noted. To put the matter simply, mistakes are unintentional and (we may assume) innocent, while abuses are intentional and culpable. Presumably, the kinds of mistakes that are in question here are those made by doctors in their diagnoses and/or prognoses. It is best just to concede up front that there will be such mistakes: patients will sometimes be misdiagnosed, and predictions about the subsequent course of their illness will sometimes be off the mark. The literature is replete with first-person accounts by patients who say something like the following: "My doctor gave me six months to live, but here I am five years later. I'm sure glad I didn't have the option of an assisted death." Mistakes will be made because doctors are human and because medicine is both art and (inexact) science.

However, there is no reason to expect more mistakes in end-of-life scenarios than in other contexts; in fact, there is reason to expect fewer since when the stakes are highest doctors are likely to be particularly careful in diagnosis and prognosis. In light of the heightened stakes, PAD policies standardly require a second opinion by an independent physician. But even with the best safeguards mistakes will still happen. And they matter more in this context for the reason noted by Kamisar: "Under any euthanasia program the consequences of mistake, of course, are always fatal." Kamisar argues that "the incidence of mistake of one kind or another is likely to be quite considerable" and then concludes that "if this indeed be the case, unless the need for the authorized conduct [that is, euthanasia] is compelling enough to override it, I take it the risk of mistake *is* a conclusive reason against such authorization."[7]

There are two issues here: the need for PAD balanced against the incidence of mistake. On the latter, Kamisar's own discussion fails to make the case that it "is likely to be quite considerable." We know from the experience of the regulatory jurisdictions that about 80% of patients who opt for PAD have been diagnosed with end-stage cancer. Kamisar himself acknowledges that "the percentage of correct diagnosis is particularly high in cancer"[8] and ends his discussion by conceding that "the incidence of error may be small in euthanasia."[9] His case against legalization really rests on the contention that the need for assisted death is not "compelling" enough to outweigh even a small likelihood of mistake. But it seems reasonable to think that the need is great on the part of the minority of dying patients whose suffering cannot be adequately controlled by other palliative measures. An acceptable policy must include safeguards designed to reduce the probability of medical error to a minimum. But it cannot be reduced to zero, and it seems cruel to deny the relief of PAD to those in need of it by insisting on medical infallibility.

In any case, the problem of mistake is no longer the one that chiefly bothers critics of legalization. John Keown, for instance, who has latterly become the most prominent of these critics, barely mentions it and then only in the context of misdiagnosis of permanent vegetative state.[10] His primary concern, and that of the others, is not mistake but abuse. Let us be clear again about the difference. A regulatory regime for assisted death is abused when its terms are intentionally (or at the very least negligently) ignored or evaded or compromised so as to yield results that those very terms do not authorize. In short, mistakes can be innocent, but abuses are culpable. So the key questions about a policy of legal PAD are as follows: In what ways might it be abused? And how likely are these abuses?

The concern about abuse often takes the form of pointing to a sector of the population who might be particularly vulnerable to abuse. Usually, that population is identified on the basis of one (or more) of the following features:

Gender. At least on the face of it, there are significant parallels between the legalization of PAD and the legalization of contraception and abortion: in both cases one of the primary arguments motivating the "pro-choice" movement appeals to self-determination or control over our lives— "our bodies, ourselves." Since feminists support women's choice when it comes to contraception and abortion, we might expect them to support the availability of safe, legal assisted death as well. Many doubtless do, but not all. Some worry that requests for PAD by women might not be genuinely autonomous or that women might be particularly susceptible to what Katrina George has characterized as "the ideal of feminine self-sacrifice."[11]

Our best evidence concerning gender patterns in PAD comes, unsurprisingly, from the legal regimes in place in Oregon and the Netherlands, both of which publish annual statistical reports. One way to determine whether women have been selectively victimized by these regimes is to compare the gender breakdown of patients who have opted for PAD with that of the general population. As George puts it, "a significantly higher incidence of voluntary euthanasia and physician-assisted suicide among women than men would suggest that women are susceptible to these practices." However, as George herself shows, the available data do not reveal a "significantly higher incidence" or, indeed, a higher incidence at all. The Dutch data (2002–13) show that 51% of total deaths have been men and 49% women. The figures for Oregon (1998–2015) are 51.4% men and 48.6% women.

It seems clear, then, that women in these jurisdictions are not electing assisted death in numbers that are out of line with their proportion of the general population.[12] Perhaps, however, women's reasons for wanting an assisted death are different from men's, reflecting the "ideal of feminine self-sacrifice." This might be the case, for instance, if women cited not wanting to be a burden to their family as a reason more frequently than men. Though studies have been done of patients' reasons for requesting assisted death, none to my knowledge have broken the results down by gender. What we do know is that among Oregon patients fear of burdening their family ranks fairly low on the list of stated reasons, well below loss of independence, loss of dignity, and wanting to control the time and manner of death.[13] It remains possible, of course, that these overall results conceal a marked gender difference, but so far we have no evidence to support this hypothesis.

Age. Might the vulnerable population be the elderly? Not according to the available data. The relevant comparison for any given age group is between its rate of assisted death and its overall death rate. In Oregon (1998–2015) 15% of all patients who died by PAS were age eighty-five or above, whereas 21% of all Oregon deaths were in this age group. About 30% were under the age of sixty-five (which is not surprising when you recall that in 80% of cases the underlying illness is cancer). In the Netherlands the rate of PAD (as a percentage of all deaths in the age group) was lowest for patients over age eighty and four times higher for those below age sixty-five.[14]

Even so, one might worry that the elderly could be particularly susceptible to coercion, subtle or otherwise, on the part of caregivers. However, it would stereotype the elderly to assume, in the absence of evidence in a particular case, that they are less able to make autonomous decisions about their end-of-life care than their younger fellows. The coercion worry might require heightened vigilance about the voluntariness of end-of-life decisions by the elderly, but presumably that would apply to all such decisions and not just the choice of assisted death.

Poverty. The poor might be disproportionately represented among patients who opt for PAD, either because they cannot afford high-quality palliative care or because they are subtly steered in that direction by physicians who prefer to treat their more affluent fellow patients. However, such data as we have do not support these hypotheses. Neither the Dutch nor the Oregon data directly report income levels for patients who die under the auspices of their policies. However, indirect measures in the Netherlands suggest that the rate of assisted death is somewhat higher for those who are better off.[15] Of course, economic status may be less of an issue in the Netherlands, with its universal health care coverage. So what about Oregon? For the period 1998–2015 only 1.4% of patients who died under the Oregon Death with Dignity Act were uninsured and

90% were already enrolled in hospice. Furthermore, they tended to be more highly educated than the state population as a whole. Ironically, the chief reason for concern about the poor might end up being exactly the opposite of the one usually voiced: if they are underrepresented among patients who opt for assisted death (as it appears they are), then perhaps they do not yet have adequate access to this service.

Race/ethnicity. The Dutch data do not include information about the race or ethnicity of patients who die by euthanasia or assisted suicide, but no suggestion has been made that the numbers are proportionally higher among the country's visible minority. In the United States race correlates highly with poverty, and there is evidence that African Americans on the whole receive less adequate medical treatment than whites.[16] The Oregon data, however, do not support the conclusion that assisted suicide is skewed toward racial or ethnic minorities. In the 1998–2015 period nearly 97% of all patients dying by PAS were white; of the remainder most were Asian and exactly one was black. Oregon, of course, does not have a large black population; it may not be safe, therefore, to extrapolate its experience to other states.

Disability. Some of the fiercest opposition to legalizing PAD has come from disability rights advocates. In the United States the national organization Not Dead Yet (named ironically after a Monty Python skit) has intervened to argue against legal assisted suicide in a number of prominent court cases as well as opposing the ballot initiatives in Oregon (1997) and Washington (2008). However, not all disability rights groups have been oppositional on this issue; in the United States AUTONOMY, Inc. has supported the legalization of assisted suicide, and in Canada an organization known as the Alliance of People with Disabilities Who Are Supportive of Legal Assisted Dying Society intervened on behalf of the plaintiffs in the *Carter* case. Opposition is also far from uniform among members of the disability community; in fact, some studies have shown that support among persons with disabilities for legalizing assisted suicide runs at roughly the same level as it does for the general population.[17]

Opponents of legalization have cited societal discrimination against persons with disabilities and the lack of acceptable alternatives available to them as reasons for doubting whether a request for assisted death by a disabled person could ever be genuinely autonomous.[18] They are also concerned that both cost-cutting considerations and devaluation of the lives of disabled persons by physicians will lead to pressures to opt for assisted death.[19] Commentators on the other side of the debate tend to acknowledge the legitimacy of these concerns but respond by arguing that characterizing persons with disabilities as incapable of autonomous decision-making simply perpetuates a negative stereotype about them and that denying them access to assisted death on that ground constitutes an objectionable form of paternalism.[20]

Attempting to determine whether the legal regimes have discriminated on the basis of disability is a tricky matter. For one thing, we need to settle on an acceptable definition of *disability*. Anita Silvers defines it as "the substantial limitation of one or more major life activities due to a physical or mental impairment" and on that basis distinguishes between disability and illness.[21] But it would seem apparent that anyone experiencing end-of-life suffering sufficiently serious to motivate a request for PAD would almost certainly qualify as disabled under this definition; after all, even extreme pain alone will substantially limit major life activities. Virtually everyone who has sought an assisted death in the Netherlands or Oregon would then be classified as disabled.

The alternative is to confine disability to something like "preexisting impairments or chronic conditions present prior to a terminal illness."[22] But in that case it becomes impossible to determine how many persons who have died under the Netherlands and Oregon policies were disabled. The Dutch data do not classify patients on the basis of their underlying condition. In Oregon, for the period 1998–2015, 8% of patients who died under the Oregon Death with Dignity Act had amyotrophic lateral sclerosis. A higher proportion of ALS sufferers sought PAD during this period than did cancer patients.[23] However, what exactly this means is anyone's guess. Is ALS (or multiple sclerosis or motor neuron disease) a disability? It is certainly common to think so, but all of these conditions are themselves fatal; they are therefore not "preexisting impairments or chronic conditions present prior to a terminal illness." So it is not clear whether the Oregon data concerning ALS have any bearing on the disability issue. Furthermore, if they do, it is also unclear what conclusion we should draw from the data. Unlike cancer, ALS tends to kill slowly, providing the patient with ample time to make a request for assisted suicide and act on it; that fact by itself may explain why a higher proportion of ALS patients than cancer patients choose to go this route.

One study of this issue using data from both the Netherlands and Oregon concluded that "there is thus no evidence that physician-assisted dying poses heightened risk to people with disabilities who are not also seriously ill."[24] The more cautious conclusion, concerning Oregon alone, is that "the issue whether [the Oregon law] disproportionately affects people with disabilities is still unresolved."[25] There is indeed no evidence of abuse on this ground, but this result is largely due to the lack of meaningful data together with the ambiguities concerning the definition of *disability*.

As mentioned earlier, the Canadian and American Supreme Court decisions of the 1990s agreed that a blanket ban on PAD was necessary in order to protect the vulnerable. We should also note that since that time the weight of judicial opinion on this question has shifted considerably, at least in Canada. After an extensive review of the evidence from foreign jurisdictions, the trial judge in the *Carter* case concluded, "The risks inherent in permitting physician-assisted death can be identified and very substantially minimized through a carefully-designed system imposing stringent limits that are scrupulously monitored and enforced."[26] A unanimous Supreme Court agreed, "The trial judge, on the basis of her consideration of various regimes and how they operate, found that it is possible to establish a regime that addresses the risks associated with physician-assisted death. We agree with the trial judge that the risks associated with physician-assisted death can be limited through a carefully designed and monitored system of safeguards."[27]

Thus far we have looked at one version of the argument from abuse, which consists of pointing to heightened risks for one or another specially vulnerable group. But it frequently takes another form, which consists of arguing that, however carefully they may be formulated and monitored, the conditions and safeguards of any policy of assisted death will inevitably be violated, to the detriment of patients. This issue of (non)compliance has tended to dominate the debate between proponents and opponents of legalization. The contested ground, the field of battle, between the two sides has been the empirical data on the operation of the PAD policies in the Netherlands and Oregon. The two sides derive their data from the same sources: annual statistical reports and peer-reviewed studies that have been done of both policies. Given the common sources, it is quite remarkable how the data have been used to support two diametrically opposed conclusions: that the policies are working just fine and that they are fatally flawed.

Rather than comb through these data yet again, we will do better to ask what could, in principle, be concluded from them concerning the incidence of abuse in either of these jurisdictions. Recall that an abuse, as opposed to a mistake, is an intentional (or at least negligent) breach of the terms of a policy that results in an assisted death that is not sanctioned by those very terms. In order to demonstrate abuse it is not enough to demonstrate noncompliance; it is also necessary to show that the safeguards in the policy were circumvented in a manner that resulted in harm to the patient. Not all instances of noncompliance, therefore, are also abuses. Perhaps the only thing that the critics and defenders of the Dutch policy have agreed on is that the reporting rate of PAD has been too low, especially in the early years. That rate stood at 80% in 2005 and has risen since. The low figures in the earlier years seem to be due in part to uncertainty on the part of physicians about the possibility of self-incrimination. Since the passage of the 2002 euthanasia law, this appears to have been less of an issue. Instead, most unreported cases seem to involve the administration of high-dose opioids (rather than the drugs recommended for euthanasia) with resulting uncertainty in the physician's mind about whether this constituted euthanasia.[28] When the opioid cases are subtracted, the reporting rate for 2005 rises to 99%. There is no similar check on the reporting rate in Oregon.

In any case, if some instances of PAD continue to be unreported, this does not by itself show that any such case involved an abuse—that the request was not genuinely voluntary or adequately informed or that the patient's suffering was not permanent and unbearable. That verdict could be rendered only by an inquiry into the case. Furthermore, it is neither reasonable nor fair to demand perfect compliance with a policy of assisted death. Some degree of noncompliance with the terms of a policy—any policy—is inevitable; that much is guaranteed by human nature. Shortcuts will be taken, safeguards will be ignored, corners will be cut.

Drawing up the appropriate regulatory framework is a balancing exercise. If we prohibit PAD entirely, then we will force some dying patients to endure needless suffering. Similarly, if we permit it but insist on airtight conditions, then the regulatory regime itself will stand in the way of effective relief for many of these patients. On the other hand, if we permit the practices with no safeguards, then we will be exposing some patients to avoidable risks. So we have to aim somewhere in the middle, at a reasonable set of safeguards to prevent most abuses, knowing full well that compliance will be imperfect. There are costs to both permitting PAD and limiting it: the permission risks harm to third parties (through abuse), and the limitation risks harm to the intended beneficiaries of the policy (by limiting access). As we raise the bar of regulation, we decrease the risk to third parties and increase it for patients; as we lower the bar, the reverse will be true. The best regulatory regime is the one with the optimal balance of these costs. No regime can eliminate all of them.

Is helping patients to die contrary to a doctor's professional duty?

The two foregoing arguments rest on the empirical claim that instituting a regime of legal PAD will inevitably have unintended, and unacceptable, consequences. We turn now to a quite different kind of argument, one that contends that providing PAD violates a duty that is specific to doctors by virtue of their role or profession. The idea of role-specific duties is itself perfectly legitimate: teachers have specific duties to their students, plumbers to their customers, politicians to their constituents. So doctors doubtless have role-specific duties as well. Could these duties include the duty not to help their patients die? Some have argued that they do.[29] This claim often fails to rise above the level of a trite slogan ("Doctors should cure, not kill") or a reference to the Hippocratic oath ("I will not give anyone a deadly drug if asked for it"). At other times it merely invokes the authority of a long tradition in which physicians have allegedly refrained from helping their patients to die.[30]

But let us assume that the claim can take a more serious and substantive form than that. If so, then it invites us to ask what the role-specific duties of a doctor are. Doubtless there are many such duties, owed to different parties (their patients, the health care institutions for which they work, their profession, their society, etc.) and with different contents (honesty, confidentiality, trust, competence, etc.). But presumably the relevant item for the present purposes is the duty of care they owe to their patients. At the most abstract level, it seems plausible to think that this duty takes two main forms: the duty to act in the patient's best interest and the duty to respect the patient's autonomy. It should be obvious that there is nothing in either duty that precludes acting on an informed request for PAD by a competent patient when that is the best means of preventing further intolerable suffering. On the contrary, it could be argued that granting a request under these circumstances is required by both duties.

We reach the same result if we invoke the familiar "Georgetown principles" for biomedical ethics.[31] The two aspects of the duty of care distinguished above invoke the principles of beneficence and autonomy, both of which are capable of supporting PAD. The principle of nonmaleficence requires physicians not to harm their patients or make their condition worse. When a patient is experiencing intolerable suffering that cannot be effectively relieved by any other end-of-life measure (short of terminal sedation), the refusal of PAD prolongs that suffering; since this has the result of making the patient's dying process worse than it needs to be, it arguably violates the nonmaleficence principle. Indeed, it can be plausibly argued that doctors have an especially stringent role-specific duty of care owed to their patients not to allow them to suffer if they have the means to prevent that suffering. Far from precluding offering patients an assisted death, the most widely accepted ethical principles governing the physician–patient relationship would seem (at least sometimes) to require it.

Perhaps, however, we are looking in the wrong place for the role-specific duties incumbent on doctors. They are, after all, professionals who are bound by the code of ethics of their profession; perhaps it is that code that prohibits assisting a patient's death. The American Medical Association takes the view that PAD "is fundamentally incompatible with the physician's role as healer," though it is noteworthy that this position statement has not been updated since 1996. It also has a Code of Medical Ethics, consisting of nine principles dealing with such issues as patient confidentiality and upholding professional standards. None of these principles seem to prohibit offering PAD to a patient who qualifies for it under the terms and conditions of a legal policy. Indeed, some of the principles might be read as permitting, or even requiring, providing this option:

I. A physician shall be dedicated to providing competent medical care, with compassion and respect for human dignity and rights.

III. A physician shall respect the law and also recognize a
responsibility to seek changes in those requirements
which are contrary to the best interests of the patient.

VIII. A physician shall, while caring for a patient, regard
responsibility to the patient as paramount.[32]

Would helping patients to die undermine the physician–patient relationship?

So it has seemed to some of the critics. Leon Kass, for example, writes, "The patient's trust in the doctor's whole-
hearted devotion to the patient's best interests will be hard
to sustain once doctors are licensed to kill."[33] Kass's worry
is that if PAD were legalized, patients would never be certain that their doctors wouldn't choose just to kill them off,
especially if they were old and poor, rather than go to the
trouble of treating them. Most doctors would, I think, be
pretty insulted by this suggestion. The vast majority of doctors, including the ones who are treating patients well advanced in the dying process, are dedicated to doing the best
they can for those under their care. It is difficult to believe
that this would change were they able to offer their patients
the option of euthanasia or assisted suicide, in addition to
all of the conventional forms of palliative care. There is no
evidence that patients in the Netherlands or Oregon trust
their doctors less than those in prohibitionist jurisdictions
or less than they did before PAD was legalized.

But Kass is also worried about the effects of legalization
on the physicians themselves: "The psychological burden
of the licence to kill (not to speak of the brutalization of the
physician-killers) could very well be an intolerably high
price to pay for physician-assisted euthanasia, especially
if it also leads to greater remoteness, aloofness, and indifference as defenses against the guilt associated with harm-
ing those we care for."[34] But are doctors in the Netherlands

or Oregon who have assisted the deaths of their patients more psychologically burdened and brutalized than doctors elsewhere, and do they now treat their patients with greater remoteness, aloofness, and indifference? Kass has provided no evidence to think so, and his speculation is not supported by studies of the effects on Dutch physicians of participating in assisted deaths.[35]

Are doctors willing to assist the deaths of their patients?

That's a fair question since no legal regime for assisted death would be viable if physicians were uniformly opposed to it and unwilling to participate in it. We know already that the American Medical Association opposes legalization of PAD. However, opposition to legalization by medical bodies is not universal in the United States. During the period prior to the vote in 1994 on Ballot Measure 16—the Oregon Death with Dignity Act—the Oregon Medical Association adopted a neutral position on the issue, while a majority of its members supported legalization.[36] By contrast, the Washington State Medical Association opposed Ballot Initiative I-1000 in 2008, despite the fact that a majority of its membership supported the measure. For the most part, colleges of physicians have also taken adverse positions. However, in October 2009 the Quebec College of Physicians called for changes in the Canadian Criminal Code to facilitate a wider variety of treatment options in end-of-life care, including euthanasia.[37] That bold step kick-started the process that led eventually to the adoption of the Act Respecting End-of-Life Care in 2015.

In any case, the opposition to assisted death by the major medical associations does not reflect a similar unanimity among their members. In a literature review of thirty-nine studies of attitudes of American physicians done between 1991 and 2000 the proportion who supported legalizing

PAE varied from a quarter to more than a half, with a slightly wider range for PAS.[38] A 2014 survey by Medscape found that 54% of physicians supported the right of a patient with an incurable illness to seek "a dignified death" (that figure was up from 46% in 2010).[39]

There have been enough studies in various countries to support the generalization that while doctors tend to be less supportive of a change in the law than the general public, they are far from uniformly opposed. Indeed, many studies show not only a significant minority in favor of legalization but, more importantly, a similar minority prepared to practice within the terms of the law should it be changed. We should keep in mind that in jurisdictions like Oregon and the Netherlands the number of patients who request assisted death is quite small and the number who follow through with it is even smaller. It may be, therefore, that only a minority of physicians will be called upon to provide the service. To put it in crude economic terms, as long as the supply is adequate to meet the demand, a legal regime for assisted death can be workable. The history of abortion teaches us that it may be one thing to change the law and quite another to ensure that the service is equally available to all who want it. Under a policy of legal assisted death there will inevitably be patients who meet the criteria but are unable to find a willing physician. Right-to-die societies, such as Compassion and Choices, may be able to help match patients and physicians, and the willingness (or otherwise) of individual doctors to provide the service may become better known over time.

Is helping patients to die consistent with the goals of palliative care?

It is not at all clear why palliative care and assisted death are sometimes thought to be antithetical.[40] As mentioned earlier (Chapter 2), the World Health Organization characterizes palliative care as "an approach that improves the quality of life of patients (adults and children) and their families who are facing problems associated with life-threatening illness. It prevents and relieves suffering through the early identification, correct assessment and treatment of pain and other problems, whether physical, psychosocial or spiritual."[41] This definition appears to leave room for a wide array of measures, all of which are aimed at "the prevention and relief of suffering" and the "treatment of pain and other problems, physical, psychosocial, and spiritual." Both PAS and PAE would seem to fit comfortably within that mandate.

Experience in the jurisdictions where these measures are legal has shown that only a small minority of patients will opt for an assisted death when offered the full spectrum of palliative measures. But for that minority, it is important that this option be available since they have come to the conclusion that nothing else on offer is managing to reduce their suffering to a tolerable level. In Oregon 90% of patients who have opted for PAS have been in hospice; for them the choice between other palliative measures and assisted death was not "either/or" but "both/and." In fact, it seems fair to say that we can't know how well the conventional palliative measures are serving the needs of dying patients until we make the option of assisted death legally available to them. There seems no reason why PAD should not be thought of as a measure of last resort within palliative care, not as an alternative to it. In Belgium we have an example in which the development of palliative care and the movement to legalize euthanasia grew up side by side, with little antagonism, and in which this model of "integral palliative care" has worked to mutual benefit.[42]

Some polls of physicians have found opposition to legalization to be strongest among palliative care specialists.

However, there is some evidence of movement on this issue. In 2007 the American Academy of Hospice and Palliative Medicine, reflecting the existence of "deep disagreement" on the issue, adopted a position of "studied neutrality" on legalization.[43] The Oregon Hospice Association opposed the Oregon Death with Dignity Act before it was adopted in 1994 and supported its repeal in 1997; now that the act is in effect the Association has no position on it, except that no Oregon hospice should turn away a patient on the ground that he or she is considering exercising his or her rights under the law.[44] It is not surprising that health care providers who work with dying patients—and the organizations that represent them—should feel especially conflicted over this issue. For one thing, should any form of PAD become legally available, they will find themselves among the doctors on the front line having to make some very difficult personal and professional decisions. In addition, any demand for PAD on the part of dying patients—especially those already in hospice—could seem like a rejection and indictment of the services provided by those who are dedicated to caring for them ("I've done my best for him, but he still insists he wants to die").

On the other hand, most palliative care physicians recognize that a minority of dying patients will experience refractory symptoms, including pain, that are not responsive to the strongest pharmacological agents (short of terminal sedation).[45] Furthermore, where PAD is legal the reasons most frequently given by patients for seeking it do not cite strictly physiological symptoms, such as pain or nausea or shortness of breath, but rather those "psychosocial and spiritual" problems noted by the World Health Organization, including a sense of meaninglessness or hopelessness, loss of independence, isolation, indignity, and inability to engage in the activities that make life worth living. While good hospice care can go some way toward alleviating these concerns, they are the forms of suffering least susceptible to a medical remedy. Patients who find them intolerable are bearing witness not to the failure of even the best conventional palliative care but to its limits.

Would legalizing PAD erode the delivery of other forms of palliative care?

This has not been the experience in the jurisdictions that have legalized assisted death. In Oregon both the rate of use of hospice facilities and the quality of hospice care appear to have risen since the passage of the Oregon Death with Dignity Act in 1994.[46] Furthermore, in Oregon the percentage of patients electing PAS who were already enrolled in hospice has increased over the years. As mentioned earlier, Belgium provides us with an example of a jurisdiction in which the provision of other end-of-life measures and euthanasia have developed together in the model of "integral palliative care." The fact that legalization of PAD and improved delivery of palliative care have gone hand in hand in these jurisdictions should not surprise us: if patients have the option of an assisted death, then doctors have a strong motive for ensuring that it is chosen truly as a last resort and not for lack of adequate end-of-life care.

The Netherlands is sometimes cited as just the opposite: a jurisdiction in which the legalization of PAD has come at the expense of the development of good-quality palliative care.[47] But this conclusion appears to be largely based on a misunderstanding about the delivery of palliative care in that country.[48] Compared to other jurisdictions, the Netherlands has traditionally had relatively few institutions—hospices—dedicated solely to the provision of palliative care. Instead, these services were for the most part provided in nursing homes, hospital units, or at home by family physicians. This situation has latterly begun to change so that as of 2006 there were two hundred specialized institutions for hospice palliative care in the country. Most palliative care, however, is still provided at home by family physicians. There is no evidence to suggest that the quality of that care is inferior to what is available in other countries; indeed, a recent "Quality of Death" index devised by the Economist Intelligence Unit ranked the Netherlands eighth out of eighty countries evaluated (just ahead of the United States).[49] Furthermore, palliative care in the Netherlands is fully covered by private or public health insurance.

Shouldn't we wait to legalize PAD until we can guarantee every dying patient high-quality palliative care?

The provision of hospice and palliative care has expanded dramatically over the past two or three decades, but we doubtless still have a considerable distance to go before every patient who needs it has access to it. PAD should be considered a legitimate last-resort option within palliative care, not an alternative to it. In that case the provision of "high-quality palliative care" should include making PAD available to those for whom the more conventional measures do not suffice. We should not think that we must choose between two policy aims: expand access to the conventionally accepted end-of-life measures or legalize assisted death. We can, and should, do both—as was done in Belgium when the Law on Palliative Care, guaranteeing patients the right to obtain information on palliative care options from their physicians, was passed in the same month (June 2002) as the Law on Euthanasia. We should also keep in mind that even the best end-of-life care will not eliminate the demand for assisted death.

Of course, the goal of ensuring the best palliative care for everyone will not be achieved overnight, especially in a period of continually expanding health care costs. But meanwhile we can't say to someone whose end-of-life suffering is so intense that they want the relief of an assisted death, "Yes, we understand that this is hard for you but, you see, not everyone yet has access to the same quality of palliative care that you have enjoyed. We realize that it has not worked for you and nothing will work but an assisted death. But you will just have to wait until we've been able to expand our palliative services to everyone who needs them." That would be unspeakably cruel.

Why do patients need doctors to help them die? Can't they just do it themselves?

It is true that at least many end-stage cancer patients could jump off a bridge, throw themselves under a subway train, hang themselves, or (the American way) shoot themselves in the head. But why would they regard any of these scenarios as a good way to die? What would the impact of any of them be on their families? Why would they choose to end their lives with an act of violence if other options were available? Wouldn't a peaceful and gentle end, with family gathered round, be better for everyone? Marcia Angell tells the story of her father, who shot himself at age eighty-one in the end-stages of prostate cancer. She concludes, "If physician-assisted suicide had been available to my father, as it is to the people of Oregon, I have no doubt that he would have chosen a less violent and lonely death."[50]

Of course, patients could try to manage this peaceful and gentle end on their own by stockpiling a supply of opiates or barbiturates until they thought they had enough to do the job. Their death would still be a lonely affair since anyone who remained with them would risk a charge of assisting a suicide. Furthermore, it is easy to make mistakes so that instead of dead they could end up brain-damaged or in an emergency room having their stomach pumped. Most patients will lack what doctors have—namely, the expertise to bring about their death efficiently and safely (that is, without unwanted side effects). Like every other end-of-life measure, this one is best managed by those who know how to do it (and have legal access to the best pharmacological means).

Why do patients need PAD when they can die by refusing food and water?

By contrast with the last question, this one at least compares PAD with another end-of-life option that can be carried out in a health care institution (very commonly a hospice) and under medical supervision. We have already seen (Chapters 2 & 5) that competent patients have the moral and legal right to refuse any form of life-sustaining treatment, including nutrition and hydration. Some have argued that the availability of this option to patients who wish to die renders legalization of assisted death unnecessary.[51] Certainly, it has some advantages. Many patients who are well advanced in the dying process lose their appetites spontaneously. Furthermore, if a patient makes a conscious decision to refuse food and fluids, carrying out this decision does not require the cooperation of any physician (on the contrary, attending physicians are required not to intervene). Finally, in prohibitionist jurisdictions it has the considerable advantage of being legal.

However, it also has serious drawbacks.[52] First, it is slow: depending on the condition of the patient, it will take anywhere from a few days to a couple of weeks for death to occur if no fluids are taken, longer if some are. Second, it is difficult or impossible to control the timing of death. This can be an important matter if a patient wishes to be able to say a final goodbye to his or her family or to have them gathered around at the end. Third, especially in the early stages the process may be attended by some discomfort (though nothing that cannot be alleviated in a medical setting). Fourth, it is not easy: it may require some degree of willpower to persist with it, at least until the body begins to shut down. Finally, some patients (and their families) may find the idea of death by dehydration repugnant. The virtues of PAD are that the process can be quick, painless, easy, and scheduled when the patient wants it. When both options are legally available, some patients will still choose to die by stopping food and water, as is their right. But others will prefer assisted death; having the former available does not eliminate demand for the latter.

9

WHAT MIGHT LIE FURTHER DOWN THE ROAD?

What is nonvoluntary physician-assisted death?

We have now surveyed all of the ethical and legal issues concerning physician-assisted death, with one major exception. Thus far we have confined ourselves to PAD that is voluntary, meaning that it is freely chosen by the patient at the time at which it is administered. Voluntariness therefore presupposes contemporaneous decisional capacity on the part of the patient, a presupposition that frequently fails in end-of-life scenarios. At least on the face of it, the voluntary/nonvoluntary distinction appears to be an ethically significant one. The case for the justifiability of all end-of-life measures so far discussed, including assisted death, has appealed to the same pair of values: well-being and autonomy. Since each of these values appears to matter a great deal by itself in ethical decision-making, any argument that is able to draw on both of them will be very powerful. When a treatment decision is nonvoluntary, appeal can still be made to the patient's best interest, but the absence of decisional capacity will preclude at least the normal kind of appeal to patient self-determination. It is therefore an open question whether measures that can be justified when voluntary can also be defended when nonvoluntary.

If we make the assumption that a patient is either de-cisionally capable or not at the time that PAD is admin-istered, then the voluntary/nonvoluntary distinction is mutually exclusive. Decisional capacity surely admits of degrees, but it must still be determined whether *this* pa-tient surmounts the threshold of capacity and is therefore to be recognized as the decision maker for *this* treatment at *this* time. And that will be a yes-or-no determination. However, the binary distinction conceals an important difference among the nonvoluntary cases. A patient who lacks current capacity may or may not have had capacity at an earlier time. We will say that a patient who has had such capacity and subsequently lost it is *formerly competent*, while a patient who has never had capacity is *never compe-tent*. The importance of this distinction lies in the fact that patients in the former category, but not the latter, may have made an end-of-life treatment decision in advance of the time it is to be put into effect. If so, then self-determination may still be in play for them as a factor in justifying the later decision either to administer or to withhold/with-draw treatment. We might think of these cases not as purely nonvoluntary but rather as quasi-voluntary, and we will discuss them first.

While there are many conditions under which deci-sional capacity may be irretrievably lost, in what follows we will focus on just two of them: permanent (irreversible) unconsciousness and advanced dementia.

Is it legal to withhold life-sustaining treatment from permanently unconscious patients?

Most jurisdictions have specific provisions governing the making and application of advance health care direc-tives. Among other things, these provisions allow sub-stitute decision makers to refuse treatment—including life-sustaining treatment—on behalf of (formerly competent but currently) incompetent patients. In the event of such refusal, health care providers are under a duty not to administer such treatment and are protected from liability for withholding or withdrawing it.

However, matters are less clear-cut when the formerly competent patient has not executed a written directive. The first high-profile case in which the American courts had to face this issue was that of Karen Quinlan, who was twenty-one when she lapsed into a permanent vegetative state in April 1975, after ingesting a combination of alcohol and tranquilizers. She was placed on a ventilator and fed through a nasogastric tube. After several months during which she remained unresponsive, her family requested that the ventilator be removed. Hospital officials refused to comply, taking the view that this step would be tantamount to killing her. Their refusal was upheld in Morris County Court on the grounds that disconnecting the ventilator would not be in Ms. Quinlan's best interest. However, this decision was overturned on appeal to the New Jersey Supreme Court, which cited her constitutional right to privacy.[1] Ms. Quinlan's ventilator was removed in May 1976, but she proved to be capable of breathing on her own. She remained in a permanent vegetative state until her death in June 1985.

The Quinlan decision was not appealed beyond the New Jersey courts, but a similar case reached the US Supreme Court in 1990. Nancy Cruzan lapsed into a permanent vegetative state in 1983 as a result of oxygen deprivation to the brain following an automobile accident. Ms. Cruzan could receive nutrition and hydration only through a feeding tube implanted in her stomach. After she had remained in this condition for several years, her parents sought and received permission from the trial court in Missouri to withdraw the feeding tube. This decision was then reversed in the

Missouri Supreme Court. The court recognized a patient's right to refuse life-sustaining treatment through the device of an advance directive. However, Ms. Cruzan had executed no written directive; instead, the trial court had heard testimony from her roommate concerning whether she would want to live or die under certain conditions. The court ruled that this testimony did not meet the standard of "clear and convincing evidence" set out in the Missouri Living Will statute. Under the substituted judgment standard, Ms. Cruzan's surrogate decision makers were obliged to base their treatment decisions on her previously expressed wishes, insofar as these could be known. Where the evidence concerning these wishes was inconclusive or equivocal, they were not entitled to refuse life-sustaining treatment on her behalf.

When this decision was appealed to the Supreme Court, the narrow issue to be adjudicated was whether the Missouri requirement of "clear and convincing evidence" was consistent with the due process clause of the Fourteenth Amendment. A divided court held that it was.[2] Following this decision, Ms. Cruzan's parents went back to the trial court with new evidence concerning their daughter's treatment wishes, which the court accepted as meeting the evidentiary standard. The feeding tube was removed, and Ms. Cruzan died in December 1990. Leaving the evidentiary issue aside, the *Cruzan* decision clearly affirmed the right of substitute decision makers to refuse life-sustaining treatment—including nutrition and hydration—for an incompetent patient on the basis of a prior refusal by the patient of that treatment.

What role should be played by advance directives?

Treatment decisions will sometimes need to be made for patients who are unable to register contemporaneous consent to (or refusal of) treatment. In that case, two questions immediately present themselves: Who should make the treatment decision? On what basis should the decision be made? Both questions are answered, in principle at least, by the standard model of advance care planning. The basic idea behind this model is simple. While you will not be capable of informed consent/refusal should you become severely demented or permanently unconscious, at an earlier stage in your life, when you are still decisionally capable, you can anticipate that you may later find yourself in one or the other of these conditions. If you wish to be able to exercise some degree of control over your later treatment, then the obvious mechanism is to register your treatment decisions in advance, ideally in a written instrument. These will be now-for-then decisions, as opposed to the normal contemporaneous now-for-now decisions. But because they are made by a decisionally capable patient, though applicable only in the event of incapacity, they will still count as the exercise of self-determination.

There are two types of instrument available for advance care planning. *Instruction directives* (also known as *living wills*) allow persons to stipulate which modes of treatment they accept and which they reject under particular conditions of incapacity (such as advanced dementia and permanent unconsciousness). In effect, they provide the opportunity to register *now* the decisions the person would make *then*, if capable of doing so. *Proxy directives* (also known as *durable powers of attorney*) appoint someone else to serve as substitute decision maker for the (later) incapacitated patient. Most advance directives include both types of instrument, in which case they provide answers to both of the foregoing questions: treatment decisions for the incapacitated patient should be made by whomever the patient has designated in advance as a proxy, and they should be made on the basis of the patient's advance instructions.

So understood, advance care planning is a logical extension of the doctrine of informed consent. Just as the requirement of informed consent safeguards the individual's autonomy in contemporaneous treatment (or nontreatment) decisions, so the requirement that advance directives be respected safeguards the individual's autonomy over such decisions at later stages of life. Furthermore, if we continue to assume that autonomous individuals are normally the best judges of their own interests, then respecting treatment (or nontreatment) decisions registered in advance will have the added justification that they are also protective of patient well-being. Every US state now makes some legislative provision for written advance directives, and several states explicitly recognize coma or permanent vegetative state as a condition that can justify withdrawal of treatment in compliance with the terms of such a directive.

The standard model of advance care planning therefore appears to provide a straightforward means whereby formerly competent patients may exercise some degree of control over their end-of-life care. That control can take the form of either requesting or refusing familiar modes of treatment: resuscitation, tube-feeding, ventilation, administration of antibiotics, sedation. Alas, however, these matters are not as simple as they might seem. From the outset critics have raised a number of concerns about reliance on advance directives for decision-making on behalf of formerly competent patients. Some of these concerns turn on issues that are specific to cases of advanced dementia, and we will come to them shortly when we discuss these cases in more detail. But some of them are more general, challenging the efficacy of advance care planning, and we will deal with them first. To keep matters as uncomplicated as possible, for the moment we will focus on advance refusals of treatment, postponing the issue of advance requests until later.

Over the past couple of decades Rebecca Dresser has been the most persistent critic of this model of advance care planning.[3] Most of her objections have been broadly practical in nature, pointing to various respects in which advance treatment refusals are less reliable than contemporaneous ones as expressions of patient self-determination. Although she does not sort them in this way, I will divide the issues she has raised into two categories: problems of information and problems of vagueness.

The informational deficiencies of advance directives are best appreciated by contrasting them with contemporaneous care decisions. One of the core elements of the doctrine of informed consent is the requirement of disclosure, the general rule of which is that the patient must be provided with all of the information that a reasonable person in his or her particular circumstances would need in order to make a reasoned decision concerning the treatment in question. This information will normally include the patient's diagnosis and prognosis in the absence of treatment (including any uncertainty attending these matters), the nature of each of the available treatment options, the probable outcome of each option, and the risks attached to each option. The requirement of disclosure requires communication, preferably face to face, between the patient and his or her health care providers, with the attendant opportunity for both questioning and discussion. Furthermore, it must be emphasized that the information is specific to *this* treatment for *this* condition and *this* patient. It can therefore be as full and detailed as the patient requires and the circumstances permit. In principle at least, contemporaneous decision-making can live up to the highest ideals of informed choice.

Contrast this rosy picture with treatment decisions made years, even decades, before the onset of incapacity and the need for treatment. Not only are there many types and degrees of incapacity (including dementia and unconsciousness) but there are even more conditions for which an incapacitated patient might require life-sustaining treatment. To try to anticipate all of these future contingencies in detail and to decide for each of them whether to accept or decline a particular form of treatment is a practical impossibility. By contrast, therefore, with the specificity of contemporaneous consent/refusal, advance decision-making is necessarily more general: for this *kind* of condition I accept/refuse this *kind* of treatment. It is also, by its nature, less susceptible to the give and take of direct communication with one's health care provider. General scenarios can, of course, be discussed in advance as hypotheticals, but doing so is far less informative than a specific treatment consultation. Finally, contemporaneous decision-making also has the advantage that the information provided is up to date. While it may not be possible to anticipate further discoveries or treatment modalities that would be relevant to the patient's decision, at least the current state of both knowledge and art can be fully communicated. By contrast, treatment decisions registered far in advance might be rendered obsolete or redundant by subsequent medical developments. Even if these decisions were as informed as possible *then*, they may not reflect the options available to the incapacitated patient *now*. For that reason they also may not reflect the informed choices the patient would make now, were he or she capable of such choices.

The informational deficiencies canvassed in the previous paragraph are all factual in nature. But it is equally possible for a person's values to shift with the passage of time so that a decision autonomously made earlier in one's life ceases to have that status later. Advance directives can, of course, be modified or renounced entirely in response to changes of heart. But for various practical reasons this may not happen, with the result that the treatment decisions re-corded in the written directive are now uninformed, not about factual matters but about the subject's own prefer-ences. Furthermore, it is often difficult, or even impossible, to anticipate in advance what it would be like to be in the various conditions for which one is trying to plan. As an active, able-bodied person you might imagine full-body paralysis, or "locked-in" syndrome, to be unendurable. When it occurs you might discover that it still makes a meaningful life possible, but if you are unable to commu-nicate treatment decisions at the time, you might find your-self bound by your own earlier, uninformed preferences.

The vagueness problem for advance directives is a corol-lary of the foregoing informational impediments. Whereas contemporaneous refusal is specific as to both treatment and occasion, advance instructions must attempt to antici-pate a wide variety of treatment options and circumstances. While one might attempt to respond to each of these pos-sible scenarios with detailed and precise directions con-cerning forms of treatment to be withheld or withdrawn, there is a strong tendency toward broader and more gen-eral directions such as "No resuscitation if I become termi-nally ill" or "No life-sustaining measures whose burdens would outweigh their benefits." Instructions as vague as these cannot be applied mechanically to later treatment decisions and therefore require interpretation by substi-tute decision makers: Does the do-not-resuscitate order apply when resuscitation would make possible six more months of meaningful life? How do we decide when the burdens of further life have become great enough to out-weigh the benefits? Indeed, instruction directives can be vaguer still, simply recording the subject's values or pri-orities for life: "I believe that life should have dignity" or "I don't want to be too much of a burden on others." In these cases advance care planning loses much of its utility in determining treatment decisions for (later) incompetent patients.

Uninformed and vague directives both raise the same basic kind of worry: that the instructions the person recorded *then*, while competent, do not adequately specify the choices he or she would make *now*, when incompetent. Of course, his or her current lack of capacity (we are assuming) makes it impossible for him or her to make an autonomous, informed decision about care. But we can still ask what he or she would decide now *were he or she capable of doing so*. If we have reason to think that his or her current (hypothetical) decision might be different from, or just underdetermined by, his or her former (actual) decision, then we have a problem: once again, on what basis are treatment decisions for incompetent (but formerly competent) patients to be made?

Broadly speaking, there appear to be three ways of answering this question, each of which has something to be said for it. The first is the one that we have already been considering: when a formerly competent patient has executed an instruction directive, then the proxy decision maker should follow the directions recorded therein. This approach will not help us in the case of any patient who has neglected to complete such a directive, though it might be extended to some whose wishes have been communicated by other, less formal means. But the practical problems noted by Dresser are sufficient to render straightforward reliance on advance directives problematic in a broad range of cases.

We need a different way of proceeding when there is no directive, when the directive is too vague to be of much use, when it is based on obsolete information, or when we have reason to believe that the patient's preferences have subsequently changed. If our primary concern is to respect patient self-determination, then the logical next step is to the *substituted judgment standard*: the proxy should attempt to make the treatment decision that the patient himself or herself would make *if he or she were capable*. The thought experiment required by this standard might seem odd, even incoherent. Here we have a patient who, *ex hypothesi*, is decisionally incapable due to some condition such as advanced dementia or permanent vegetative state. Any treatment decisions made for such a patient must, presumably, take into account his or her current condition. Yet we are asked to imagine what decision he or she would make *were he or she decisionally capable*—that is, *were he or she not in this condition*. Under those circumstances, he or she would presumably have no reason to forgo life-sustaining treatment, but what does that tell us about his or her wishes for his or her actual condition? Perhaps the way around this conundrum is something like the following. We are to imagine that, miraculously, this demented or unconscious person has been restored to temporary lucidity, during which time we can ask how he or she wishes to be treated once he or she lapses back into the demented or unconscious state. Then the substituted judgment standard tells the proxy decision maker to follow the directions the patient would provide under such conditions.

If we adopt this standard for all treatment decisions on behalf of incompetent (but formerly competent) patients, including those with written directives, then the role of advance directives becomes essentially evidentiary: a subject's directive gives us evidence—more or less reliable, depending on the circumstances, but rarely conclusive—concerning the decisions he or she would now make if capable. The problems of information and vagueness pressed by Dresser are not sufficient to undermine the evidentiary role of advance directives on a substituted judgment standard. Even a vaguely worded directive provides some insight into a person's deeply held values and goals for the end-stage of life. If our aim is to respect the patient's autonomy over his or her treatment decisions, then a written directive must be given serious evidentiary weight. At the same time, the evidence that it provides concerning his or her current (hypothetical) decision must also be rebuttable—by reasons for thinking that his or her recorded refusal of treatment was based on misapprehensions about his or her current condition, by subsequent indications that his or her values may have changed, by new and salient information about treatment options, or whatever.

Advance directives therefore have an important role to play—albeit an evidentiary one—under a regime of substituted judgment. We have not yet, however, dealt with the full force of Dresser's critique of reliance on directives, which is not (merely) practical but normative. Dresser's principal concern is with cases in which following a patient's advance directive would conflict with that patient's own present interests. Competent individuals are, of course, entitled to refuse treatment when doing so will be worse for them: Jehovah's Witnesses may do this when they decline blood transfusions, and anyone can decline treatment on altruistic grounds (for example, so as not to unduly burden his or her family). When we honor these refusals, as we often must, we effectively side with patient autonomy over patient well-being.

Since the point of the substituted judgment standard is also to respect patient autonomy, there is so far no obvious reason why we should not equally honor advance refusals that conflict with present interests. But Dresser argues that there are special problems in the case of an advance refusal by a (formerly) competent person that, if respected, would be contrary to the best interest of the (later) incompetent patient. In such cases, she urges, we should reject substituted judgment in favor of the *best interest standard*:

the proxy decision maker should attempt to make the treatment decision that is in the patient's best interest. On this standard, advance directives diminish even further in significance as guides to decision-making for incompetent patients, though they may still tell us something about how the patient views—or once viewed—his or her interests.

The conflict that Dresser envisages requires that the patient have current interests that will be compromised if the instructions in an advance directive are carried out. Arguably, however, this cannot be the case for patients who, like Nancy Cruzan, have become permanently unconscious. Recalling the earlier discussion of these issues (Chapter 1), two facts about Nancy are relevant: (1) under any reasonable criteria for determining death, she is alive; (2) almost certainly, she has only biological life and no personal life. (We must say "almost certainly" here because there have been some cases of successful communication with permanent vegetative state [PVS] patients.)[4] Since it seems unlikely that bare biological life has any value for the person who is living it (Chapter 4), it is difficult, if not impossible, to find any respect in which continued life is in the best interest of a patient like Nancy. Dresser's concerns, then, become most acute when we are dealing not with the permanently unconscious but with the severely demented. We will return to them when we come to consider these cases. But first a piece of unfinished business concerning PVS patients like Nancy Cruzan.

Is there a case for euthanasia for permanently unconscious patients?

Cruzan's parents petitioned the courts for the right to remove her feeding tube. Very commonly it is said that their purpose in doing so was to allow her to die. However, it seems equally accurate to say that (1) their intention was to cause Nancy's death and (2) the cause of her death was dehydration as a result of the removal of the tube. In that case, what the court allowed them to do was to intentionally cause their daughter's death. An injection of a lethal medication would also have intentionally caused Nancy's death. If the removal of the feeding tube was justified, then it seems that physician-assisted euthanasia in Nancy's case would have been equally justified (had it been legally available). Since we are assuming that Nancy's life no longer had any value for her, neither alternative could be contrary to her interests. But then if patients can register advance refusals of life-sustaining treatment (including food and fluids), why should they not be able to register advance requests for euthanasia? *Ex hypothesi*, the difference between these options would make no difference to Nancy. But for the family it could have made a considerable difference since they could have given Nancy a quick release at the time of their choosing rather than having to watch her waste away for nearly two weeks.

This suggests that a policy of legal PAD should allow for advance euthanasia requests, at least for certain kinds of future incapacity. Because the Oregon law authorizes only physician-assisted suicide and not PAE, there is no room in it for advance requests. (Unconscious patients cannot orally ingest medication.) The question therefore becomes more acute for jurisdictions that also permit PAE. The Dutch euthanasia law contains the following provision: "If the patient aged sixteen years or older is no longer capable of expressing his will, but prior to reaching this condition was deemed to have a reasonable understanding of his interests and has made a written statement containing a request for termination of life, the physician may carry out this request."[5] Advance euthanasia directives can therefore technically be binding in the Netherlands. We must say "technically" here since there have been few, if any, actual cases of PAE on the basis of such a directive since the passage of the law in 2002. It is not difficult to see why. Immediately following the passage quoted above, we find the statement, "The requirements of due care, referred to in the first paragraph, apply *mutatis mutandis.*" Those requirements include the physician's determination that "the patient's suffering was lasting and unbearable." At least in the case of a permanently unconscious patient, it is difficult to see how this condition could be satisfied, even *mutatis mutandis*.

The Belgian law contains a narrower provision for advance euthanasia directives specifically targeting PVS patients like Nancy Cruzan: "In cases where one is no longer able to express one's will, every legally competent person of age, or emancipated minor, can draw up an advance directive instructing a physician to perform euthanasia if the physician ensures that: (1) the patient suffers from a serious and incurable disorder, caused by illness or accident; (2) the patient is no longer conscious; and (3) this condition is irreversible given the current state of medical science."[6] To date, about 2% of euthanasia cases in Belgium have fallen under this provision. There is no similar provision for advance euthanasia directives in the case of persons with dementia.

What about patients suffering from dementia?

To see how dementia cases can be much more problematic, it will be helpful to work with the example introduced and discussed by Ronald Dworkin:

> When Andrew Firlik was a medical student, he met a fifty-four-year-old Alzheimer's victim whom he called Margo, and he began to visit her daily in her

apartment, where she was cared for by an attendant. The apartment had many locks to keep Margo from slipping out at night and wandering in the park in a nightgown, which she had done before. Margo said she knew who Firlik was each time he arrived, but she never used his name, and he suspected that this was just politeness. She said she was reading mysteries, but Firlik "noticed that her place in the book jumps randomly from day to day; dozens of pages are dog-eared at any given moment. . . . Maybe she feels good just sitting and humming to herself, rocking back and forth slowly, nodding off liberally, occasionally turning to a fresh page." Margo attended an art class for Alzheimer's victims—they all, including her, painted pretty much the same picture every time, except near the end, just before death, when the pictures became more primitive. Firlik was confused, he said, by the fact that "despite her illness, or maybe somehow because of it, Margo is undeniably one of the happiest people I have ever known." He reports, particularly, her pleasure at eating peanut-butter-and-jelly sandwiches.[7]

Dworkin invites us to imagine that years before, when she was fully competent, Margo gave considerable thought to the overall course of her life and reached the settled conviction that she never wanted to live as a demented person; perhaps she regarded such a life, however happy it might be, as undignified or demeaning. (If we wish, we can also imagine that Margo's assessment of such a life was informed by her experience of her mother's final years.) Acting on this conviction, she executed an instruction directive declining all life-sustaining treatment in the event that she should reach the advanced stages of Alzheimer's. Now she has acquired an infection easily treatable by antibiotics but fatal if left untreated. Should her earlier refusal of treatment be respected, allowing her to die despite the evident fact that she is now quite happy?

Dworkin contends that it should, on grounds of both Margo's autonomy and her well-being. He argues that, due to her dementia, Margo is no longer capable of making autonomous decisions about how her life should go. But she was once capable of such decisions—indeed, made just such a decision—and respect for her precedent autonomy requires doing now what she then directed. Thus far, we might seem to have another case of conflict between autonomy and well-being: respect for Margo's autonomy will require us to do what is worse for her, namely, allow her to die. But Dworkin resists this construal of the situation, arguing that honoring Margo's advance refusal may also be in her overall best interest. He supports this contention with a distinction between two types of interest, which he calls *experiential* and *critical*. Our experiential interests consist of the pleasure or enjoyment we take in things that we do or that happen to us. Margo has always had experiential interests and still does since she gives every sign of enjoying her mystery book, her art class, and her peanut-butter-and-jelly sandwiches. Allowing her to die would be contrary to her current experiential interests.

Critical interests, on the other hand, are based on a person's convictions of how life should go and the goods it should contain. Margo's critical interests, Dworkin argues, were formed by her past convictions about the overall course of her life, including her wish not to finish it as a demented person. Margo is now unable to form critical interests, Dworkin claims, since she now lacks the capacity to think about the overall course of her life, but she retains the critical interests she formed while previously competent. Postponing her death by giving her life-sustaining treatment would be contrary to those interests. Since

Dworkin considers that, in case of conflict, critical interests should be given priority over experiential interests, he concludes that, all things considered, honoring Margo's advance refusal would best serve her well-being (as well as her autonomy).

Rebecca Dresser disagrees with Dworkin about this case in two important respects. First, because she advocates a best interest standard of decision-making for patients like Margo, she rejects the contention that we are bound to respect Margo's (precedent) autonomy. Second, she argues that in applying the best interest standard only Margo's current experiential interests should be considered, in which case the decision should be made to prolong her life, at least as long as she continues to be happy. Clearly, this second claim is crucial to her view since if she were to acknowledge that Margo's critical interests are also in play, then the best interest standard she favors might entail complying with Margo's advance refusal of life-sustaining treatment. Dresser puts her point in the following way: "Happy and contented Margo will experience clear harm from the decision that purports to advance the critical interests she no longer cares about. This seems to me justification for a policy against ... withholding effective, nonburdensome treatments, such as antibiotics, from dementia patients whose lives offer them the sorts of pleasures and satisfactions Margo enjoys."[8] Presumably, the decision to withhold treatment will cause "clear harm" only to Margo's experiential interests. Why, then, are we not also to consider her critical interests? Dresser's answer to this question is—and must be—that they no longer matter because "she no longer cares about" them. She develops this point at greater length in a later discussion:

> If a patient can no longer appreciate the values that
> motivated the [advance] choice, treatment decisions

should take into account what now matters to the patient. When the capacity to appreciate critical interests is lost, experiential interests should take priority. Competent persons are free to elevate their critical interests above experiential interests. But after they lose decisional capacity, they have a different set of concerns. Experiential interests become central to their lives. Experiential interests should also be central to decisions about their life-sustaining treatment.[9]

In other words, if you are no longer capable of caring about your critical interests, then those interests do not count.

Dresser provides no real defense for this contention, and it is difficult to see how it could be defended. If you once accept Dworkin's notion of critical interests—which Dresser does—and if these interests include a person's settled conviction about how the end-stage of life should go, what reason could there be for discounting these interests simply because the person has later lost the capacity to endorse, or even understand, them? It would be a different matter if, at some stage before or during the gradual onset of her dementia, Margo had reconsidered and disavowed her earlier disparagement of life in a demented condition. In that case there would be no reason to consider her earlier view of the matter still authoritative as an expression either of her autonomy or of her interests. But we are to suppose that she neither reconsidered nor disaffirmed her refusal of treatment when she was still capable of doing so. Now that she has lost this capacity her earlier directions remain our only evidence of where her current critical interests lie. Indeed, disregarding these interests because she has now lost the capacity to appreciate them would seem to undermine the whole point of advance care planning. If I execute an instruction directive while competent, then my aim in doing so is to direct my care when I become incompetent. It would be perverse to disregard my earlier directions simply because I am now in the very condition of incapacity I anticipated in recording them.

It should now be clear why permanent unconsciousness provides a simpler case than dementia for advance refusals of treatment (and, needless to say, for advance requests for euthanasia). Though Margo undeniably has (in Dworkin's terms) experiential interests while in her demented condition, Nancy has none. In Margo's case we have a conflict of interest, with her experiential interests providing a reason for and her critical interests providing a reason against prolonging her life. There is no such conflict of interest for Nancy, so her family and health care providers need not feel similarly conflicted about acting on her wishes.

Actually, the situation is a little more complicated than that. Because "disorders of consciousness" are difficult to diagnose with certainty, in a small minority of instances patients mistakenly diagnosed as PVS subsequently regain consciousness.[10] In light of this fact, one commentator has argued that as long as there is a nonzero probability of the patient recovering consciousness, then his or her best interest requires sustaining life; he or she cannot be worse off that way (since, subjectively, unconsciousness and death are indistinguishable for him or her) and he or she might be better off (since he or she might recover consciousness).[11] However, this argument assumes that we are to consult only the patient's experiential interests. Just to complicate matters even further, functional magnetic resonance imaging of PVS patients has shown that a small percentage of them have some capacity for awareness and cognition and, in some cases, even communication by means of brain activity.[12] This last, fascinating, result opens up the intriguing possibility of consulting some PVS patients concerning their care. However, it should be stressed that this seems to apply only to a very small minority of "permanently unconscious" patients with traumatic brain injury and not at all to cases like that of Nancy Cruzan, whose unconsciousness was precipitated by oxygen deprivation to the brain.

Despite the differences between dementia and disorders of consciousness, we should not lose sight of the important factor they have in common: if we accept Dworkin's framework, then in each case we have at least a provisional reason, based on respect for both patient autonomy and patient well-being, for complying with the advance directive. Whether this reason is conclusive will depend on a number of factors. For one thing, the various practical problems raised by Dresser should lead us to treat a written directive as a presumptive indication of the subject's settled convictions about his or her care, subject to rebuttal by evidence of informational deficits, later change of heart, or other factors.

But there are other complicating factors in the dementia scenario as well. Agnieska Jaworska has argued that at least mid-stage dementia patients (such as Margo) are capable of both having and, to a lesser extent, acting on values and that this capacity for valuing is all that is necessary in order to have both critical interests and a rudimentary form of autonomy.[13] If Jaworska is right, then the decision to comply with Margo's advance refusal of treatment is not, as Dworkin argued, settled by respecting her precedent autonomy and her critical interests. Instead, there will be both critical interests and expressions of autonomy manifested during her dementia that must also be part of the equation. In that case, her proxy decision makers will need to decide whether to attach more weight to her earlier (fuller) autonomy and (more autonomous) critical interests or her later (diminished) autonomy and (less autonomous) critical interests, as well as determining how to balance all of these factors against her current experiential interests. It would be entirely understandable if, rather than attempting to sort out these deep philosophical questions, they simply opted to continue life support for Margo as long as she remained happy.

Let us recapitulate the argument to this point. We began with a simple and straightforward case in favor of advance care planning as a means of extending patient self-determination over periods of incapacity. We then considered Rebecca Dresser's practical objections to advance directives, followed by her more philosophical arguments that (a) in deciding on behalf of incompetent patients we should reject the substituted judgment standard in favor of the best interest standard and (b) in applying this standard we should confine our attention to current experiential interests. Though, taken together, these two contentions would effectively negate the authority of advance refusals of treatment, we did not find reason to accept either of them.

To this point we have been assuming that advance directives for dementia patients like Margo take the form of selective refusal of various life-sustaining procedures. Suppose instead that Margo had registered an advance request for euthanasia, to be carried out in the event that she became severely demented. (Again, we will assume that PAE is legal in her jurisdiction.) We would then have to decide whether to honor this expression of precedent autonomy or, if we chose to work with the substituted judgment standard, whether her advance request constituted credible evidence of her current hypothetical choice. If we put Margo's interests in play, under a best interest standard, then we will once again have to balance her critical against her experiential interests. But we had to engage all of these issues when her instruction directive took the form of refusing life-sustaining treatment. Nothing of ethical significance appears to change when, instead, it takes the form of requesting life-terminating treatment. Actually, that is not quite true: ending Margo's life quickly and painlessly by means of a lethal injection might be better for her, and those who care about her, than allowing her to die by an untreated infection.

Can we actually imagine administering euthanasia to happy and contented Margo? The foregoing argument yields only a comparative judgment: if honoring Margo's advance refusal of life-sustaining treatment is justifiable, then so is honoring her advance request for euthanasia. Euthanasia directives therefore introduce no novel entries into the ethical balance sheet. But perhaps, like Dresser, we cannot imagine ourselves acting on either directive in the face of Margo's current contentment with her (diminished) life. Our reluctance to do so might just be perspectival error: we are confronted daily by Margo's current experiential enjoyments, whereas her previous disparagement of the life she is now living seems barely visible in the distant past.

If we wish to give our reluctance some philosophical support, then the obvious means would be to agree with Dresser in rejecting Dworkin's privileging of critical over experiential interests. As a general thesis, it is hard to see how one might argue that current pleasures and enjoyments, under conditions of diminished or nonexistent autonomy, always take precedence over previous, fully autonomous expressions of one's deepest and most enduring values. However this might be, it is well to keep in mind that Margo is the easiest case for Dresser's rejection of advance directives and the hardest case for Dworkin's defense of them. Mid-stage Alzheimer's is seldom as rosy as Margo's day-to-day experience, and the end-stages of the disease never are. As patients slide further and further into dementia, it is far more common for their lives to be marked by disorientation, irritability, and episodes of aggression or rage. In these cases current experiential interests no longer speak so unequivocally in favor of prolonging life, and the case for acting on an advance refusal/request becomes stronger. In order to dismiss reliance on advance directives altogether for patients with dementia, Dresser would have to contend that we could never have a sufficient reason for honoring a directive, however distressed the person had become. No such sweeping claim seems at all plausible.

What about infants?

End-of-life decisions that hasten death are easiest to justify when the twin values of self-determination and well-being are both in play. This is paradigmatically the case when these measures are fully voluntary, the outcome of the patient's contemporaneous informed consent. However, there remains room for appeal to both values in the case of a patient who, while currently incompetent, has previously had decisional capacity since reference back to his or her earlier values and preferences (with or without an explicit advance directive) can help us to determine both what he or she would now choose, if able, and what would now be in his or her best interest. These important pieces of evidence are, however, entirely absent in cases in which the patient has never had decisional capacity. These are, accordingly, the cases in which treatment (or nontreatment) decisions hastening death are hardest to justify.

Some persons lead lives, often lengthy ones, during which they never manifest decisional capacity. One such was Joseph Saikewicz, who had a lifelong IQ of ten and a mental age of approximately two years and eight months. When Mr. Saikewicz was sixty-seven years old he was diagnosed with acute myeloblastic monocytic leukemia, which is invariably fatal and which, if left untreated, would lead to death in a matter of weeks or months. Administration of chemotherapy would offer some hope of temporary remission, at best only a few months, and would be accompanied by severe adverse side effects. The decision was made by his court-appointed guardian not to initiate this treatment.[14]

An even more dramatic instance of permanent incapacity is found in the Canadian case of Tracy Latimer, who suffered from a severe form of cerebral palsy caused by neurological damage at the time of her birth. She was quadriplegic, had the mental capacity of a four-month-old baby, suffered frequent seizures, and experienced considerable pain as her spine and joints were distorted by the gradual but inexorable tightening of her muscles. She underwent numerous surgeries intended to correct these problems. When she was twelve years old and scheduled for further surgery to deal with a dislocated hip, her father killed her by means of carbon monoxide poisoning in order, he said, to spare her further suffering.[15] He was convicted of second-degree murder.[16]

In both of these cases a decision was made that had the effect (and, at least in the latter case, was made with the intent) of hastening death, yet in neither of them could this decision be justified by any reference back to the person's earlier, competent wishes. So we need to ask how, if at all, these decisions could be justified. This is exactly the kind of question on the table in this section, but we will not pursue it for either the Saikewicz or the Latimer case. Instead, we will turn attention to a different class of cases that are, if anything, even more difficult: life-and-death decisions for infants.

Unlike Joseph Saikewicz and Tracy Latimer, most of us are decisionally capable through most, if not all, of our adult lives. However, we do not achieve this capacity suddenly; instead, it is developed gradually, the expectation being that (except in pathological cases) its more or less mature form will be in place by the age of majority. This gradual process leaves us with a lengthy gray area, extending roughly from the age of eleven or twelve to eighteen or nineteen, during which decisional capacity may be neither clearly present nor clearly absent. These cases of so-called mature minors can raise complex questions that need to be resolved on a case-by-case basis: To what extent is *this* person competent to consent to, or refuse, *this* treatment? As we saw earlier (Chapters 5 & 6), some jurisdictions, such as Belgium and the Netherlands, make some allowance for PAD decisions by patients under the age of eighteen, depending on their decisional capacity. Everyone agrees, however, that there is a lower age limit to even partial, or underdeveloped, capacity. When treatment decisions need to be made for young children (below the age of ten, let us say), the normal mechanisms of informed consent/refusal are inapplicable. On this sliding scale infants, and especially newborns, represent the extreme case.

Most newborns do not present difficult treatment decisions: either they require no treatment at all (aside from standard care) or what they need is routine and trivial or it is more serious but there is no legitimate reason not to proceed with it. However, some infants are born with disabilities, ranging from moderate to severe, that raise more challenging questions concerning their care. A severely disabled newborn may require intervention in order to sustain life, ranging from aggressive (surgery, intubation) to more routine (resuscitation, antibiotics). Decisions must therefore be made whether to initiate, withhold, continue, or withdraw any of these forms of treatment. Two questions immediately present themselves: Who should make the decision? On what basis should it be made?

On the face of it, there is a simple and obvious answer to each of these questions. Since the infant is incapable of making health care decisions, the task must fall to one or more substitute decision makers. And since the infant is also incapable of appointing a proxy, the substitute decision makers will normally be the next of kin—the parents. The basis for their decision cannot be either an advance directive or the substituted judgment standard since there is no expression of precedent autonomy, formal or informal, on which the decision makers can rely. They must therefore fall back on the best interest standard—more particularly, they must aim to make the treatment decision that is in the best interest of the child.

Each of these answers is at least partially correct. But the issues raised by the two questions are more complicated than these simple answers would suggest. We will postpone further exploration of the "Who decides?" question until later in order to come to grips first with the difficult issue of determining the best interest of a newborn. Let us start with a normal, healthy baby and ask why continuing to live would be good for him or her—or, alternatively, why dying would be bad for him or her. The obvious answer is given by the deprivation account of the badness of death that we encountered earlier (Chapter 1): dying would deprive the infant of a life worth living. If we are asked what makes a life worth living, we can help ourselves again to Ronald Dworkin's distinction between experiential and critical interests. The former include goods such as pleasure and enjoyment (and presumably the avoidance of bads such as pain and suffering). The latter include the formation of personal values and the pursuit and achievement of life goals and ambitions (and presumably the avoidance of disappointments and frustrations). Because the infant is sentient, he or she already has experiential interests, though they are currently limited to such basic matters as food, warmth, rest, and the avoidance of pain. However, as he or she matures, he or she will develop other, more complex experiential interests as well as critical interests. If he or she is even moderately fortunate, the resultant goods in life will outweigh the bads so as to render it, on the whole, worth living. Death will deprive him or her of this worthwhile life—ergo, allowing him or her to die (or killing him or her) would be bad for him or her and sustaining his or her life would be good for him or her.

The normal, healthy infant is, of course, the easy case; here we do not hesitate to offer life-sustaining treatment, if we are able. Many of the most difficult treatment/nontreatment dilemmas arise for extremely premature babies (those born before the end of the second trimester) because of the difficulty of determining the infant's prognosis (survival with only mild to moderate disabilities, survival with severe disabilities, or death). However, we will not deal with these cases but will instead focus on three of the more frequently discussed disorders that may afflict full-term infants.

Anencephaly is a neural tube defect that results in the absence of all higher-brain regions including the cerebrum, which is responsible for thinking and coordination. Infants born with anencephaly are usually blind, deaf, and unconscious. Although some individuals with anencephaly may be born with a rudimentary brainstem, the lack of a functioning cerebrum permanently rules out the possibility of ever gaining consciousness. Most newborns with anencephaly do not survive infancy; if not stillborn, then the infant will usually die within a few hours or days after birth. The anencephalic infant occupies the opposite end of the spectrum from the normal infant; by virtue of being irreversibly unconscious, he or she has no current experiential interests and no prospect of developing any future interests, whether experiential or critical. Except for lacking precedent autonomy, and therefore critical interests, the anencephalic infant is in the same condition as the PVS patient. Although his or her life contains no bads, it also contains no (present or future) goods; subjectively, it is indistinguishable from being dead. Since recovery of consciousness in this case is impossible, it cannot be contrary to the infant's interest to die. Death cannot be worse for him or her than continued life and may be better for the anguished family. In this case, therefore, there is no point in undertaking any measures to preserve life; instead, it may be that the sooner death occurs the better.

All of the hard cases lie between these extremes of normality and anencephaly. Actually, some of them are not that hard. Down syndrome is a chromosomal disorder caused by the inheritance of an extra twenty-first chromosome. Individuals with the syndrome have a characteristic set of facial features, various other physical anomalies, and lower than average cognitive ability. During the 1970s and into the 1980s there were a number of highly publicized incidents of Down syndrome infants being "allowed to die" by means of withholding treatment.[17] Most Down infants require no more neonatal care than their chromosomally normal fellows. However, in some cases the syndrome is accompanied by a physical anomaly such as a congenital heart defect or a blockage somewhere in the gastrointestinal tract. Normally, these defects are easily correctable by surgery, but they would be fatal if left uncorrected. Undertaking the corrective surgery would be a routine decision in the case of a normal infant. However, in the case of some Down infants, the needed surgery was refused by the parents, either in accordance with or contrary to medical advice. In those instances the babies were given only comfort care, including pain medication, and left to die of starvation or dehydration.

Many people were outraged that Down infants were being treated (or, better, left untreated) in this manner.

Down syndrome is a broad-spectrum disorder, with the resulting degree of cognitive impairment ranging from mild to severe and with an array of possible further complications including hearing deficits, cataracts, thyroid dysfunctions, and skeletal problems. The severity of any of these problems, including the cognitive impairment, is impossible to forecast at birth. However, what is known is that the syndrome does not result in any significant degree of suffering, save for the social stigmatization that inevitably results from looking and acting "different." In fact, the vast majority of Down infants, children, adolescents, and adults are markedly happy and content, perhaps more so than the general population. High-functioning Down adults are capable of gainful employment and living fairly independent lives. In Dworkin's terms, they definitely have experiential interests, and if we accept Jaworska's threshold for having values and exercising autonomy, they have critical interests as well. No serious case can be made that their lives are not, on balance, worth living. Accordingly, if treatment decisions are to be based on the best interest of the child, there can be no justification for withholding from Down infants any treatment that would be offered to a chromosomally normal baby.

However, we have assumed to this point that the only interests implicated by the best interest standard are those of the patient—in this case, the infant. But what of the interests of the parents or, more broadly, of the family (if other siblings are involved)? Many, perhaps most, Down children are integrated into loving families who are happy to have them. But raising a Down child undeniably imposes additional burdens on the family, especially when the degree of physical and mental disability is severe. The additional burdens of care, which will tend to fall largely on the mother, can lead to fatigue and burnout and can also strain the family's financial resources. Parents of disabled children have a higher rate of marital breakup, and the siblings of such children are more likely to be behaviorally disturbed, the incidence of disturbance correlating with the degree of the disability.[18]

Down syndrome can, of course, be diagnosed prenatally through procedures such as amniocentesis, and the vast majority of couples who receive the diagnosis will then elect abortion. What, then, are we to make of parents who discover only at birth that their infant has the condition and conclude that they will just not be able to handle the burdens of raising a Down child or that it will place too much of a strain on their other children? To what extent should these interests also be considered when applying the best interest standard? On the one hand, no parents can be compelled to raise a disabled child against their will; any such compulsion would scarcely be in the interest of the child. On the other hand, the rights of the parents extend only as far as refusing to take on the responsibility of caring for the child; they do not include refusing treatment necessary to sustain the child's life. What this means, then, is that if the parents of a Down infant elect to abandon the child, then some other arrangement—fostering, adoption, institutionalization, or whatever—must be found for him or her. While the interests of the parents will inevitably have a profound effect on the child's future circumstances, in the treatment decision itself the best interests of the child must be paramount. Since a Down infant will have a life worth living, there can be no justification for allowing him or her to die of neglect.

These matters become considerably more complicated when we turn to spina bifida, a developmental birth defect caused by the incomplete closure of the embryonic neural tube. Like Down syndrome, spina bifida encompasses a wide range of disorders. In its mildest form its physical manifestations may be virtually unnoticeable and it will result in no cognitive impairment. However, in its most severe (myelomeningocele) manifestation the spinal cord is exposed, with the result that spinal fluid leaks through the opening and the baby is prone to life-threatening infections. In these cases there will inevitably be some degree of paralysis and loss of sensation below the level of the spinal cord defect—the higher the level of the defect, the more severe the associated nerve dysfunction and resultant paralysis. In addition, bladder and bowel function may be lost and intense pain may occur, originating in the lower back and continuing down the leg. Most infants born with myelomeningocele will also have hydrocephalus, which consists of excessive accumulation of cerebrospinal fluid in the ventricles of the brain. The buildup of fluid puts damaging pressure on the brain, causing moderate to severe cognitive impairment. Like Down syndrome, spina bifida is readily diagnosable at birth and reasonably reliable estimates can be made of the expected degree of physical—but not mental—impairment.

During the 1960s and 70s a lively debate was waged among pediatricians and pediatric surgeons over the appropriate treatment of newborns diagnosed with spina bifida.[19] Some defended the view that active treatment to repair the physical defects should be undertaken for all such infants. At a minimum the corrective surgery involved would include closing the spinal column and inserting a shunt to drain the excess fluid from the brain; additional surgeries might also be needed to deal with further orthopedic anomalies, such as dislocation of the hips. The case for this treatment regime rested on the seemingly reasonable principle that every child deserved the best care available, despite the degree of disability. The problems with it came to light when follow-up studies were done of a population of infants who had been aggressively treated in this manner.[20] What was discovered was that despite the treatment only about half of these children survived, most of them dying in their first year, and that most of those who did survive past that point were severely physically disabled. Many also experienced moderate to severe mental retardation. In light of these results some physicians began to advocate a more selective approach in which infants born with the most severe disabilities would be left untreated. The aim of this regime was to reserve corrective treatment exclusively for those spina bifida infants whose prognosis was that they would suffer no worse than moderate handicap. Children who were denied treatment were offered ordinary feeding but nothing else: no incubators, no oxygen, no tube-feeding, no antibiotics. All of these children would die within six months.

The logic underlying the selective treatment regime was that spina bifida infants who present at birth with the worst physical anomalies are very likely to die in their first year of life even with maximal treatment, in which case treatment should be regarded as futile. Worse, not only would corrective treatment be of no benefit to the child but the additional suffering caused by the required surgical interventions would arguably be a harm to the child. The ethical justification for the selective approach was therefore that it would enable parents and physicians alike to identify the cases in which initiating treatment would not be in the best interest of the child. Implementing it, of course, required developing criteria for determining which infants would be denied treatment. These criteria would look to such matters as "the size and location of the opening over the spine, the existence of severe paralysis or spinal deformity, very bad hydrocephalus, and other major defects or brain damage."[21] The precise formulation of these criteria can no doubt be a matter of legitimate disagreement, especially since the criteria must be applied in the first days of the infant's life, but that is a conversation that must be left to the specialists.

In the years that have followed this debate the selective treatment regime has become the norm for newborns presenting with severe disabilities.[22] It is intended to answer one important question concerning these infants: Is this an instance in which initiating (or continuing) treatment would not be in the best interest of the child since it would have little or no chance of gaining the child a life worth living? We have seen already that the answer to this question is "yes" for anencephalic infants, and we can henceforth assume that it is also "yes" for some spina bifida (but not Down syndrome) infants. However, the first question inevitably leads to a second: What is to be done with the infants who are denied treatment? Until recently, there has been only one possible answer to this question: the infants will be given comfort care (food, water, pain medication if necessary), but no other measures will be undertaken to prolong their lives. In other words, they will be left to die. But now, at least in one jurisdiction, there is another possibility.

The Netherlands has a history of euthanasia for severely disabled infants that now stretches back more than two decades. The first case involved Dr. Henk Prins, a gynecologist who in March 1993 ended the life of four-day-old baby Rianne, born with spina bifida and hydrocephalus, resulting in severe brain damage. Dr. Prins believed that surgery on the baby would be futile and that she would suffer unbearably. After consulting with a number of colleagues, all of whom agreed with his prognosis, and with the concurrence of the parents, he administered a lethal injection. The District Court accepted his defense of necessity on the grounds that (a) the baby's suffering had been hopeless and unbearable and there had not been another medically responsible way to alleviate it, (b) both the decision-making leading up to the termination of life and the way in which it was carried out had satisfied the requirements of careful practice, (c) his behavior had been consistent with scientifically sound medical judgment and the norms of medical ethics, and (d) termination of life had taken place at the express and repeated request of the parents as legal representatives of the baby. His acquittal was upheld by the Court of Appeals. Similarly, in April 1994, with the agreement of the parents, Dr. Gerard Kadijk terminated the life of a twenty-four-day-old infant with trisomy 13 (a serious chromosomal anomaly incompatible with survival). The baby appeared to be in severe pain after brain tissue had protruded from her skull, and death was expected within six months. Like Dr. Prins, Dr. Kadijk pleaded necessity at trial, was acquitted, and had his acquittal upheld by the Court of Appeals.

The trials of Drs. Prins and Kadijk effectively established a number of legal principles in the Netherlands concerning nonvoluntary euthanasia: (a) despite the requirement of an explicit patient request in the prosecutorial guidelines for euthanasia, such a request is not necessary in order to invoke the defense of necessity; (b) the crucial factor triggering such a defense is the presence of unbearable suffering for which no alternative treatment is available; and (c) in cases of such suffering it is not worse, and arguably is better, to actively terminate life rather than to allow the patient to die. However, the case law by itself did not provide doctors with sufficient guidance in order to determine when they might be prosecuted, so once again the need for generally accepted guidelines presented itself.

Where infants were concerned this need was met by the Groningen Protocol, developed in 2002 by doctors at the University Medical Center in Groningen, with the assistance of a local prosecutor, and published nationwide in 2005.[23] The criteria for euthanasia embodied in the protocol include (a) hopeless and unbearable suffering on the part of the infant, coupled with prognosis of a very poor quality of life; (b) confirmation of the foregoing by at least one independent physician; (c) informed consent by both parents; and (d) performance of the procedure in accordance with the accepted medical standard. The protocol was subsequently adopted by the Dutch Pediatric Association for national use. Under its terms physicians are required to record the death as an unnatural one and submit a full report of each case to a national committee of experts, which will then decide whether the criteria have been met and make "recommendations" to the prosecutorial authorities. Following the protocol does not guarantee that the physician will not be prosecuted; however, it was developed on the basis of a survey of twenty-two cases reported to prosecutors over the preceding seven years, in none of which was a prosecution initiated. Needless to say, Dutch criminal law governing nonvoluntary euthanasia has not been changed; the protocol relies entirely on the by now familiar device of guidelines for prosecutorial discretion. In this respect nonvoluntary euthanasia in the Netherlands is currently in much the same situation as voluntary euthanasia was before the law reform of 2002.

Decisions not to initiate treatment in the case of some severely disabled newborns are made in every jurisdiction. But there is one important difference in the Netherlands: infants selected for nontreatment may not be left to die but rather may have their lives ended by euthanasia. Largely because of this additional feature, the protocol has been very controversial. However, there has been something quite remarkable about this controversy. The critics have focused almost exclusively on the criteria embedded in the protocol, especially the required judgment of poor quality of life and intractable suffering. One of them has concluded, after some discussion of the nature of suffering, that "it is unreasonable to believe that either a physician or parent can accurately judge whether the burdens of an infant's life outweigh the benefits of living *for that child*."[24] This claim can, of course, be contested. But what makes it remarkable is that it is so beside the point. The innovation in the protocol is not that it requires judgment calls about the prospects of severely compromised newborns; the necessity of making such calls is accepted virtually everywhere. What is novel in the protocol is the use of euthanasia for infants selected for nontreatment instead of waiting for them to die of their condition. The main points the critics make could just as easily be directed against the criteria for nontreatment that have been in place for more than thirty years now. From the point of view of the interests of the child, there may be a case against euthanasia rather than waiting for the infant to die since it precludes the possibility of an unexpectedly positive outcome. But this case would have to be weighed against the advantage of euthanasia in preventing any further suffering by the child (and, one might add, the parents). In the end, the best course of action for a particular infant will have to be determined by the particular circumstances of the case. But it should be clear by now that once the decision has been made that this infant's life is not to be rescued, there can be no objection in principle to ending the life by means of a lethal injection rather than waiting for the baby to die over a period of weeks or months. In many instances, if not all, this will be the most humane thing to do.

In the case of severely disabled newborns, the best interest standard can therefore lead to the result that (a) no corrective treatment will be undertaken for the infant's condition and (b) euthanasia will instead be administered. In short, it can justify nonvoluntary euthanasia as an outcome. Our only remaining question is the one we set aside earlier in this discussion: Who decides whether or not this baby will live? By now the broad outline of an answer to this question has already emerged. The parents are the default substitute decision makers for the child, with the authority to consent to or refuse treatment on the child's behalf. However, in the kinds of hard cases we have been discussing, parents will be dependent on the neonatal intensive care unit for expert medical opinion and advice. This dependency will inevitably result in a collaborative decision-making process between the parents and the attending physicians. When they are in agreement there will normally be no reason to overrule their mutual decision, unless (as in some of the earlier Down syndrome cases) an infant with clear prospects of a worthwhile life is being left to die. In the event that they disagree, matters become more complicated. Typically, the disagreement takes one of two forms: either the parents are refusing treatment that the health care team thinks will be of medical benefit to the infant or they are demanding treatment that the team judges to be futile.

In these cases of stalemate between parents and physicians (or hospital) there may be no recourse other than reference to some decision-making body—perhaps a hospital ethics committee in the first instance and, if the disagreement persists, ultimately a court. If the parents' refusal of treatment is found to be clearly contrary to the interests of the child, then decision-making authority may need to be transferred to a neutral party (a child services agency, a court-appointed guardian, etc.). As mentioned earlier, parents cannot be compelled to raise a seriously (or even mildly) disabled child against their will, but their refusal to care for the child cannot be a reason to deny it treatment that is judged to be clearly beneficial to it. On the other hand, if the parents are demanding life-sustaining measures that will have the effect merely of prolonging the baby's hopeless condition, then at some point the medical team may no longer have any obligation to comply with their wishes. Each case will, of course, feature its own peculiar set of circumstances so that generalizations about outcomes would be foolhardy. All that can be said with certainty in these cases is that the best interest of the child must remain paramount. Tragically, as we have seen, that interest is not always best served by continued life.

10

HOW MIGHT LEGALIZATION
BE ACHIEVED?

What kind of legal regime should advocates aim for?

The main business of this book is done. We have explored
the nature, history, and ethics of physician-assisted death
and the case that can be made for and against allowing it
as a legal end-of-life option. By now most of you will have
made up your mind on both the ethical and legal issues (if
you had not already done so before picking up the book).
If you have decided that PAD is morally wrong and should
not be legally permitted, then this final chapter is not for
you. But if you are at least open to the possibility of legalization, then a crucial further question remains to be
answered.

Earlier (Chapter 6) we examined the various shapes
that a policy of legal PAD might take. The choice among
them will doubtless be guided in part by ethical considerations, including compassion for patients at the end of
life and respect for their autonomy. However, there are
also practical questions to take into account in deciding
which regime you will seek to realize. One such question is which policy would be the best fit for the social/
political/economic conditions in your particular jurisdiction. For one thing, different jurisdictions have quite
different systems for health care delivery and health

insurance coverage. These differences may well make a difference, perhaps by making a policy that presupposes long-standing physician–patient relationships (like that in the Netherlands) more or less appropriate or by raising or lowering the concern that PAD might be promoted as a cost-saving measure. In response to considerations like these, one commentator who favors law reform has argued that the nature of health care delivery (and coverage) in the United States makes it advisable to aim at legalizing only physician-assisted suicide and not physician-assisted euthanasia.[1]

Additionally, calculations need to be made of what is politically possible. For many people a legal regime for PAS appears to be a more attractive option than one for PAE, despite the fact that there is no significant ethical difference between the two practices. It is noteworthy that ballot initiatives to legalize both forms of PAD failed in Washington (1991) and California (1992), while initiatives to legalize PAS alone succeeded in Oregon (1994 and 1997), Washington (2008) and Colorado (2016). These social/political realities might argue for focusing, at least initially, on securing a regulatory regime for PAS (perhaps modeled on the Oregon policy), reserving until later the further task of broadening it to include PAE.

The second question concerns not the objective of local law reform efforts but the means. Even if advocates agree on the policy whose implementation they wish to seek, they must still decide how best to bring it about. This question belongs properly to political strategy or tactics, or possibly political science, rather than political philosophy. Even if the same policy were (more or less) appropriate for all of the currently prohibitionist jurisdictions, the most effective strategy for putting it in place is bound to vary with local social, political, and legal conditions. Broadly speaking, there appear to be four options available.

What role might be played by legislatures?

In a representative democracy policy decisions on important matters affecting the interests of the populace should ideally be made by elected legislators. Law reform by this route has a number of significant advantages. A legislative initiative will put the issue of PAD up for debate in the public forum, where arguments on both sides of the question can be posed and assessed. Such an initiative can have the benefit of expert drafting and vetting by government lawyers, especially in the design of safeguards against abuse. A legislative committee examining a draft bill can arrange public consultations to facilitate input by interest and advocacy groups. Elected representatives will have ample opportunity to canvass the opinions of their constituents before deciding whether to support such a bill. Finally, and most importantly, a policy passed into law by this means will face no challenges to its legitimacy; opponents may seek to defeat or repeal it on some future occasion, but they cannot credibly claim that its enactment has thwarted or bypassed established democratic procedures.

However, the legislative route also faces some formidable obstacles. Like abortion, PAD is a divisive and emotionally powerful issue, capable of galvanizing strong opinions on both sides. Unless under intense pressure for change, governments are normally reluctant to stir up opposition and risk a backlash of outrage on the part of influential interest groups. The politically astute strategy is to avoid dealing with these issues unless compelled to do so. PAD is therefore likely to remain an issue that governments would rather avoid if at all possible.

Of the various legal regimes, the legislative route was the one followed in Switzerland, Belgium, Luxembourg, Vermont, and (most recently) California. Since the mid-1990s bills to legalize PAD (usually PAS, on the Oregon model) have been introduced in more than half of the US state legislatures, with success thus far only in two cases. As noted earlier (Chapter 7), public opinion on this issue in the United States as a whole shows a solid majority in favor of law reform. However, criminal law is under state jurisdiction, and some states are much more liberal on this issue than others.

What role might be played by courts?

Legal positivists are fond of reminding us that courts have the function of making law as well as applying it. There are two distinct ways in which they can shape policy concerning PAD. In a constitutional democracy a supreme court may be empowered to strike down legislation that is found to violate constitutionally entrenched rights. This is what happened in Colombia in 1997 and Canada in 2015. However, similar challenges to the laws prohibiting PAD have failed in the United States (1997) and the United Kingdom (2002).

The probability of success with any further court challenges in these jurisdictions is rather low, though in 2015 the Canadian Supreme Court did reverse its earlier 1993 decision upholding the assisted suicide law. The advantages of a successful constitutional challenge are obvious since the goal of law reform can then be achieved without the need for all that messy political action; this was the result when state laws prohibiting abortion were struck down in the United States in 1973. However, for that very reason court decisions of this sort will also elicit complaints of unwarranted "judicial activism" and the bypassing of the democratic process. Furthermore, courts are better equipped to remove existing legislation than to craft its replacement. Few think that PAD should be legally permitted with no oversight or regulation. Once the existing law has been invalidated, therefore, it becomes the task of the legislature to construct the appropriate regulatory regime. But legislators are not always eager to rise to this challenge (*vide* Colombia and Montana).

Sustaining a constitutional challenge is, however, only one way in which the courts can shape policy. The other is through the accumulation of case law as prosecutions for euthanasia or assisted suicide succeed or fail. It was via this route that PAE (and *a fortiori* PAS) was gradually legalized in the Netherlands during a period of nearly thirty years before the process culminated with a formal change in the law in 2002. Early on, the Dutch courts recognized necessity as an available defense against a charge of consensual homicide, and a sequence of acquittals (or convictions with token penalties) effectively determined the guidelines to be followed by prosecutors in deciding when to proceed with a charge. Though the politicians eventually came on board, it is fair to say that the Dutch policy of legal PAD was primarily the product of judicial, and not legislative, action.

It is doubtful that the same route could succeed in other jurisdictions. Few cases of PAS or PAE involving physicians ever come to court, and when they do the charge is frequently reduced to a more minor offense (possibly in order to avoid a challenge to the law). However, a related tactic might stand a better chance of success. During the 1970s and 1980s Dr. Henry Morgentaler was prosecuted on four separate occasions for openly defying the then existing abortion law in Canada. At trial he invoked the defense of necessity. Though it was highly doubtful that this defense was legally available to him, the argument did succeed in convincing the jurors that Dr. Morgentaler had acted in good faith and out of a genuine concern for his patients. All four juries refused to convict. As a result of these acquittals, the abortion law became virtually unenforceable, at least in Quebec, until it was finally struck down on constitutional grounds in 1988. This kind of "jury nullification" might well occur now if a physician were to be prosecuted for homicide or assisting a suicide and if the jurors could be convinced that he or she had acted out of compassion for his or her patient. A similar possibility in the United States is that a grand jury might refuse to prefer an indictment. This was the outcome in the well-known case of Dr. Timothy Quill, who published an account of the assistance he provided for the suicide of one of his patients.[2] Although his actions were the subject of a criminal investigation and Dr. Quill and other witnesses testified before a grand jury, no indictment was forthcoming.

Finally, we should note the rather special case of Montana, where the courts played a different, but equally pivotal, role in establishing a legal regime. In her 2008 decision Judge McCarter of the First Judicial District Court ruled that the state's prohibition of PAS violated rights to individual privacy and dignity guaranteed by the state constitution. So far, then, this looks like another successful constitutional challenge. However, upon appeal the Montana Supreme Court overruled Judge McCarter's constitutional decision but also found that nothing in state law prohibited assisting a suicide.[3] This is a precedent that seems unlikely to be followed in other states.

What role might be played by prosecutors?

Legislators make criminal law, and judges apply it—but only when cases are brought to them by public prosecutors. Because some degree of discretion must be employed to determine when a case is worth proceeding with, the prosecution service is another juncture in the system at which at least some instances of assisted death can be effectively legalized. The prosecution service played this role in the Netherlands from the 1970s to the formal legal amendment of 2002. Driven primarily by the court decisions in which the defense of necessity had been accepted, the Board of Procurators General worked out with the Royal Dutch Medical Association a set of guidelines whose observance would insulate physicians from legal action. Similar guidelines for the exercise of prosecutorial discretion were developed by the British Columbia attorney general following the PAS of Sue Rodriguez in 1994. More recently, the director of public prosecutions in the United Kingdom has published guidelines for cases of assisted suicide, though they are aimed primarily at determining when to proceed with a charge against family members or friends rather than physicians.[4]

Like law reform by judicial fiat, prosecutorial discretion can determine a legal regime for PAD without the need for formal legislative action. However, for this very reason it also has several drawbacks. Because the guidelines are likely to be vague and subject to interpretation, it can be very difficult for physicians (or laypersons) to determine when they will be safe from prosecution. The legal regime will also be unstable since the guidelines could be revised, or withdrawn entirely, at any time. Finally, there are limits to the exercise of prosecutorial discretion since if carried too far, the guidelines will amount to a substantive change in the law, which is the exclusive prerogative of the legislature.

What role might be played by referenda?

If democracy is defined as the political system in which decision-making is ultimately exercised by the collective citizenry, then its purest expression is the referendum. It is by this means that the assisted suicide policies were installed in Oregon (1994 and 1997), Washington (2008), and Colorado (2016). Since these policies were put to a direct vote, there can be no doubt of their political legitimacy. Furthermore, referenda are by their nature responsive to public opinion on sensitive issues like PAD, overcoming the problem that the people may be more receptive to legalization than their elected representatives and sidestepping the necessity of persuading any political party to commit to the reform agenda. Having said that, a referendum is not an ideal mechanism for the adoption of policies that, due to their subject matter, are inevitably complex and nuanced. The process provides no opportunity for careful clause-by-clause deliberation about the provisions to be built into the policy since the electorate has only the option of taking or leaving the draft legislation on offer. Furthermore, public opinion on matters such as this can be quite volatile and subject to hijacking by interest groups with little reluctance to engage in inflammatory rhetoric.

However, this avenue remains open in the twenty-one US states (besides Oregon, Washington, and Colorado), as well as the District of Columbia, where citizen-sponsored ballot initiatives are permitted; in those jurisdictions, despite its defects, the referendum route may represent the reformers' best hope, building on the original success in Oregon and the subsequent exporting of the Oregon model next door to Washington.

APPENDIX: THE OREGON DEATH WITH DIGNITY ACT

Language as appeared on Oregon Ballot Measure 16 (1994)
(ORS 127.800-897. Implemented: October 27, 1997)

Section 1

General provisions

1.01 Definitions

The following words and phrases, whenever used in this Act, shall have the following meanings:

(1) "Adult" means an individual who is 18 years of age or older.
(2) "Attending physician" means the physician who has primary responsibility for the care of the patient and treatment of the patient's disease.
(3) "Consulting physician" means the physician who is qualified by specialty or experience to make a professional diagnosis and prognosis regarding the patient's disease.
(4) "Counseling" means a consultation between a state licensed psychiatrist or psychologist and a patient for the purpose of determining whether the patient is suffering from a psychiatric or psychological disorder, or depression causing impaired judgment.
(5) "Health care provider" means a person licensed, certified, or otherwise authorized or permitted by the law of this State to

administer health care in the ordinary course of business or practice of a profession, and includes a health care facility.

(6) "Incapable" means that in the opinion of a court or in the opinion of the patient's attending physician or consulting physician, a patient lacks the ability to make and communicate health care decisions to health care providers, including communication through persons familiar with the patient's manner of communicating if those persons are available. Capable means not incapable.

(7) "Informed decision" means a decision by a qualified patient, to request and obtain a prescription to end his or her life in a humane and dignified manner, that is based on an appreciation of the relevant facts and after being fully informed by the attending physician of:
(a) his or her medical diagnosis;
(b) his or her prognosis;
(c) the potential risks associated with taking the medication to be prescribed;
(d) the probable result of taking the medication to be prescribed;
(e) the feasible alternatives, including, but not limited to, comfort care, hospice care, and pain control.

(8) "Medically confirmed" means the medical opinion of the attending physician has been confirmed by a consulting physician who has examined the patient and the patient's relevant medical records.

(9) "Patient" means a person who is under the care of a physician.

(10) "Physician" means a doctor of medicine or osteopathy licensed to practice medicine by the Board of Medical Examiners for the State of Oregon.

(11) "Qualified patient" means a capable adult who is a resident of Oregon and has satisfied the requirements of this Act in order to obtain a prescription for medication to end his or her life in a humane and dignified manner.

(12) "Terminal disease" means an incurable and irreversible disease that has been medically confirmed and will, within reasonable medical judgment, produce death within six (6) months.

Section 2

Written request for medication to end one's life in a humane and dignified manner

2.01 Who may initiate a written request for medication

An adult who is capable, is a resident of Oregon, and has been determined by the attending physician and consulting physician to be suffering from a terminal disease, and who has voluntarily expressed his or her wish to die, may make a written request for medication for the purpose of ending his or her life in a humane and dignified manner in accordance with this Act.

2.02 Form of the written request

(1) A valid request for medication under this Act shall be in substantially the form described in Section 6 of this Act, signed and dated by the patient and witnessed by at least two individuals who, in the presence of the patient, attest that to the best of their knowledge and belief the patient is capable, acting voluntarily, and is not being coerced to sign the request.

(2) One of the witnesses shall be a person who is not:
    (a) A relative of the patient by blood, marriage, or adoption;
    (b) A person who at the time the request is signed would be entitled to any portion of the estate of the qualified patient upon death under any will or by operation of law; or
    (c) An owner, operator, or employee of a health care facility where the qualified patient is receiving medical treatment or is a resident.

(3) The patient's attending physician at the time the request is signed shall not be a witness.

(4) If the patient is a patient in a long term care facility at the time the written request is made, one of the witnesses shall be an individual designated by the facility and having the qualifications specified by the Department of Human Resources by rule.

Section 3

Safeguards

3.01 Attending physician responsibilities

The attending physician shall:

(1) Make the initial determination of whether a patient has a terminal disease, is capable, and has made the request voluntarily;

(2) Inform the patient of:
   (a) his or her medical diagnosis;
   (b) his or her prognosis;
   (c) the potential risks associated with taking the medication to be prescribed;
   (d) the probable result of taking the medication to be prescribed;
   (e) the feasible alternatives, including, but not limited to, comfort care, hospice care, and pain control.

(3) Refer the patient to a consulting physician for medical confirmation of the diagnosis, and for determination that the patient is capable and acting voluntarily;

(4) Refer the patient for counseling if appropriate pursuant to Section 3.03;

(5) Request that the patient notify next of kin;

(6) Inform the patient that he or she has an opportunity to rescind the request at any time and in any manner, and offer the patient an opportunity to rescind at the end of the 15 day waiting period pursuant to Section 3.06;

(7) Verify, immediately prior to writing the prescription for medication under this Act, that the patient is making an informed decision;

(8) Fulfill the medical record documentation requirements of Section 3.09;

(9) Ensure that all appropriate steps are carried out in accordance with this Act prior to writing a prescription for medication to enable a qualified patient to end his or her life in a humane and dignified manner.

3.02 Consulting physician confirmation

Before a patient is qualified under this Act, a consulting physician shall examine the patient and his or her relevant medical records and confirm, in writing, the attending physician's diagnosis that the patient is suffering from a terminal disease, and verify that the patient is capable, is acting voluntarily, and has made an informed decision.

3.03 Counseling referral

If in the opinion of the attending physician or the consulting physician a patient may be suffering from a psychiatric or psychological disorder, or depression causing impaired judgment, either physician shall refer the patient for counseling. No medication to end a patient's life in a humane and dignified manner shall be prescribed until the person performing the counseling determines that the person is not suffering from a psychiatric or psychological disorder, or depression causing impaired judgment.

3.04 Informed decision

No person shall receive a prescription for medication to end his or her life in a humane and dignified manner unless he or she has made an informed decision as defined in Section 1.01(7). Immediately prior to writing a prescription for medication under this Act, the attending physician shall verify that the patient is making an informed decision.

3.05 Family notification

The attending physician shall ask the patient to notify next of kin of his or her request for medication pursuant to this Act. A patient who declines or is unable to notify next of kin shall not have his or her request denied for that reason.

3.06 Written and oral requests

In order to receive a prescription for medication to end his or her life in a humane and dignified manner, a qualified patient shall have made an oral request and a written request, and reiterate the oral request to his or her attending physician no less than fifteen (15) days after making the initial oral request. At the time the qualified patient makes his or her second oral request, the attending physician shall offer the patient an opportunity to rescind the request.

3.07 Right to rescind request

A patient may rescind his or her request at any time and in any manner without regard to his or her mental state. No prescription for medication under this Act may be written without the attending physician offering the qualified patient an opportunity to rescind the request.

3.08 Waiting periods

No less than fifteen (15) days shall elapse between the patient's initial and oral request and the writing of a prescription under this Act. No less than 48 hours shall elapse between the patient's written request and the writing of a prescription under this Act.

3.09 Medical record documentation requirements

The following shall be documented or filed in the patient's medical record:

(1) All oral requests by a patient for medication to end his or her life in a humane and dignified manner;

(2) All written requests by a patient for medication to end his or her life in a humane and dignified manner;

(3) The attending physician's diagnosis and prognosis, determination that the patient is capable, acting voluntarily, and has made an informed decision;

(4) The consulting physician's diagnosis and prognosis, and verification that the patient is capable, acting voluntarily, and has made an informed decision;

(5) A report of the outcome and determinations made during counseling, if performed;

(6) The attending physician's offer to the patient to rescind his or her request at the time of the patient's second oral request pursuant to Section 3.06; and

(7) A note by the attending physician indicating that all requirements under this Act have been met and indicating the steps taken to carry out the request, including a notation of the medication prescribed.

3.10 Residency requirements

Only requests made by Oregon residents, under this Act, shall be granted.

3.11 Reporting requirements

(1) The Health Division shall annually review a sample of records maintained pursuant to this Act.

(2) The Health Division shall make rules to facilitate the collection of information regarding compliance with this Act. The information collected shall not be a public record and may not be made available for inspection by the public.

(3) The Health Division shall generate and make available to the public an annual statistical report of information collected under Section 3.11(2) of this Act.

3.12 Effect on construction of wills, contracts, and statutes

(1) No provision in a contract, will, or other agreement, whether written or oral, to the extent the provision would affect whether a person may make or rescind a request for medication to end his or her life in a humane and dignified manner, shall be valid.

(2) No obligation owing under any currently existing contract shall be conditioned or affected by the making or rescinding of a request, by a person, for medication to end his or her life in a humane and dignified manner.

3.13 Insurance or annuity policies

The sale, procurement, or issuance of any life, health, or accident insurance or annuity policy or the rate charged for any policy shall not be conditioned upon or affected by the making or rescinding of a request, by a person, for medication to end his or her life in a humane and dignified manner. Neither shall a qualified patient's act of ingesting medication to end his or her life in a humane and dignified manner have an effect upon a life, health, or accident insurance or annuity policy.

3.14 Construction of act

Nothing in this Act shall be construed to authorize a physician or any other person to end a patient's life by lethal injection, mercy killing, or active euthanasia. Actions taken in accordance with this Act shall not, for any purpose, constitute suicide, assisted suicide, mercy killing, or homicide, under the law.

Section 4

Immunities and liabilities

4.01 Immunities

Except as provided in Section 4.02:

(1) No person shall be subject to civil or criminal liability or professional disciplinary action for participating in good faith compliance with this Act. This includes being present when a qualified patient takes the prescribed medication to end his or her life in a humane and dignified manner.

(2) No professional organization or association, or health care provider, may subject a person to censure, discipline, suspension, loss of license, loss of privileges, loss of membership, or other penalty for participating or refusing to participate in good faith compliance with this Act.

(3) No request by a patient for or provision by an attending physician of medication in good faith compliance with the

provisions of this Act shall constitute neglect for any purpose of law or provide the sole basis for the appointment of a
guardian or conservator.

(4) No health care provider shall be under any duty, whether by
contract, by statute, or by any other legal requirement, to participate in the provision to a qualified patient of medication
to end his or her life in a humane and dignified manner. If
a health care provider is unable or unwilling to carry out a
patient's health care request, and the patient transfers his or
her care to a new health care provider, the prior health care
provider shall transfer, upon request, a copy of the patient's
relevant medical records to the new health care provider.

4.02 Liabilities

(1) A person who without authorization of the patient willfully
alters or forges a request for medication or conceals or destroys a rescission of that request with the intent or effect of
causing the patient's death shall be guilty of a Class A felony.

(2) A person who coerces or exerts undue influence on a patient to
request medication for the purpose of ending the patient's life,
or to destroy a rescission of such a request, shall be guilty of a
Class A felony.

(3) Nothing in this Act limits further liability for civil damages
resulting from other negligent conduct or intentional miscon-
duct by any persons.

(4) The penalties in this Act do not preclude criminal penalties
applicable under other law for conduct which is inconsistent
with the provisions of this Act.

Section 5

Severability

5.01 Severability

Any section of this Act being held invalid as to any person or cir-
cumstance shall not affect the application of any other section of

this Act which can be given full effect without the invalid section or application.

Section 6

Form of the request

6.01 Form of the request

A request for a medication as authorized by this Act shall be in substantially the following form:

REQUEST FOR MEDICATION TO END MY LIFE IN A HUMANE AND DIGNIFIED MANNER

I, _____, am an adult of sound mind.

I am suffering from _____, which my attending physician has determined is a terminal disease and which has been medically confirmed by a consulting physician.

I have been fully informed of my diagnosis, prognosis, the nature of medication to be prescribed and potential associated risks, the expected result, and the feasible alternatives, including comfort care, hospice care, and pain control.

I request that my attending physician prescribe medication that will end my life in a humane and dignified manner.

INITIAL ONE:

____ I have informed my family of my decision and taken their opinions into consideration.

____ I have decided not to inform my family of my decision.

____ I have no family to inform of my decision.

I understand that I have the right to rescind this request at any time.

I understand the full import of this request and I expect to die when I take the medication to be prescribed.

I make this request voluntarily and without reservation, and I accept full moral responsibility for my actions.

Signed: _____

Dated: _____

DECLARATION OF WITNESSES

We declare that the person signing this request:

(a) Is personally known to us or has provided proof of identity;

(b) Signed this request in our presence;

(c) Appears to be of sound mind and not under duress, fraud, or undue influence;

(d) Is not a patient for whom either of us is attending physician.

_____ Witness1/_____ Date

_____ Witness2/_____ Date

Note: One witness shall not be a relative (by blood, marriage, or adoption) of the person signing this request, shall not be entitled to any portion of the person's estate upon death, and shall not own, operate, or be employed at a health care facility where the person is a patient or resident. If the patient is an inpatient at a health care facility, one of the witnesses shall be an individual designated by the facility.

NOTES

Preface

1. Andrew Dugan, "In U.S., Support Up for Doctor-Assisted Suicide," Gallup, May 27, 2015, http://www.gallup.com/poll/183425/support-doctor-assisted-suicide.aspx. Accessed June 10, 2016.

2. "Aging Statistics," Administration on Aging, Administration for Community Living, last modified May 24, 2016, http://www.aoa.acl.gov/Aging_Statistics/Index.aspx. Accessed June 10, 2016.

3. Atul Gawandi, *Being Mortal: Medicine and What Matters in the End* (New York: Metropolitan Books, 2014).

4. L. W. Sumner, *Assisted Death: A Study in Ethics and Law* (Oxford: Oxford University Press, 2011).

Chapter 1

1. Ad Hoc Committee of the Harvard Medical School, "A Definition of Irreversible Coma," *Journal of the American Medical Association* 205, no. 6 (1968): 337–40.

2. Lucretius, "On the Nature of Things," in *The Stoic and Epicurean Philosophers: The Complete Extant Writings of Epicurus, Epictetus, Lucretius, Marcus Aurelius*, ed. Whitney J. Oates (New York: Modern Library, 1940), 131.

3. "Deaths and Mortality," National Center for Health Statistics, Centers for Disease Control and Prevention, last modified

June 20, 2016, http://www.cdc.gov/nchs/fastats/leading-causes-of-death.htm. Accessed October 8, 2016.

4. "Where Do Americans Die?," Stanford School of Medicine, https://palliative.stanford.edu/home-hospice-home-care-of-the-dying-patient/where-do-americans-die/. Accessed June 10, 2016.

Chapter 2

1. World Health Organization, *Palliative Care*, Fact Sheet no. 402, http://www.who.int/mediacentre/factsheets/fs402/en/. Accessed October 8, 2016.

2. Nuremberg Tribunal, "The Nuremberg Code," in *Doctors of Infamy: The Story of the Nazi Medical Crimes*, ed. A. Mitscherlich and F. Mielke (New York: Schuman, 1947), xxiii–xxv.

3. Allen Buchanan and Dan W. Brock, *Deciding for Others: The Ethics of Surrogate Decision Making* (Cambridge: Cambridge University Press, 1989), 52–55.

4. J. L. Bernat, B. Gert, and R. P. Mogielnicki, "Patient Refusal of Hydration and Nutrition—An Alternative to Physician-Assisted Suicide or Voluntary Active Euthanasia," *Archives of Internal Medicine* 153, no. 24 (1993): 2723–28.

5. See, e.g., Fred Rosner, "Why Nutrition and Hydration Should Not Be Withheld from Patients," *Chest* 104, no. 6 (1993): 1892–96.

6. The position of the American College of Physicians is typical: "Artificial administration of nutrition and fluids is a medical intervention subject to the same principles of decision making as other treatments"; *ACP Ethics Manual*, 6th ed., https://www.acponline.org/clinical-information/ethics-and-professionalism/acp-ethics-manual-sixth-edition-a-comprehensive-medical-ethics-resource/acp-ethics-manual-sixth-edition. Accessed October 8, 2016.

7. M. Siegler and A. Weisbard, "Against the Emerging Stream: Should Fluids and Nutritional Support Be Discontinued?," *Archives of Internal Medicine* 145, no. 1 (1985): 129–31.

8. Floyd Angus and Robert Burakoff, "The Percutaneous Endoscopic Gastrostomy Tube: Medical and Ethical Issues

in Placement," *American Journal of Gastroenterology* 98, no. 2 (2003): 272–77.

9. Susan Anderson Fohr, "The Double Effect of Pain Medication: Separating Myth from Reality," *Journal of Palliative Medicine* 1, no. 4 (1998): 319.

10. Timothy E. Quill, "Principle of Double Effect and End-of-Life Pain Management: Additional Myths and a Limited Role," *Journal of Palliative Medicine* 1, no. 4 (1998): 334.

11. Ibid.

12. See, e.g., M. Maltoni, et al., "Palliative Sedation Therapy Does Not Hasten Death: Results from a Prospective Multicenter Study," *Annals of Oncology* 20, no. 7 (2009): 1163–69.

Chapter 4

1. The best contemporary source for this view is John Finnis, *Natural Law and Natural Rights* (Oxford: Clarendon Press, 1980), chs. 3–4.

2. Ibid., 118–25.

3. Ibid., 86.

4. John Finnis, "A Philosophical Case Against Euthanasia," in *Euthanasia Examined: Ethical, Clinical and Legal Perspectives*, ed. John Keown (Cambridge: Cambridge University Press, 1995), 32–33.

5. Jonathan Glover, *Causing Death and Saving Lives* (Harmondsworth, UK: Penguin Books, 1977), 45–46.

6. Ibid., 52.

7. Alan Donagan, *The Theory of Morality* (Chicago: University of Chicago Press, 1977), sec. 2.4.

Chapter 5

1. *Schloendorff v. Society of New York Hospital*, 211 NY 125 (1914).

2. Nuremberg Tribunal, "The Nuremberg Code," in *Doctors of Infamy: The Story of the Nazi Medical Crimes*, ed. A. Mitscherlich and F. Mielke (New York: Schuman, 1947), xxiii–xxv.

3. *Bouvia v. Superior Court*, 225 Cal. Rptr. 297 (Cal. App. 2 Dist. 1986).

4. *Nancy B. v. Hôtel-Dieu de Québec et al.*, 86 D.L.R. (4th) 385 (1992).

5. *Vacco et al. v. Quill et al.*, 117 S. Ct. 2293 (1997).

6. Swiss Penal Code [*Schweitzerisches Strafgesetzbuch*], trans. Lara Pehar, https://www.admin.ch/opc/de/classified-compilation/19370083/index.html. Accessed October 4, 2016.

7. Swiss National Advisory Commission for Biomedical Ethics (NEK-CNE), *Assisted Suicide: Opinion No. 9/2005* (Bern: NEK-CNE, 2005), 7 (emphasis in original).

8. Ibid., 56.

9. Stephen J. Ziegler and Georg Bosshard, "Role of Non-Governmental Organisations in Physician Assisted Suicide," *British Medical Journal* 334, no. 7588 (2007): 295.

10. Elke M. Baezner-Sailer, "Physician-Assisted Suicide in Switzerland: A Personal Report," in *Giving Death a Helping Hand: Physician-Assisted Suicide and Public Policy, an International Perspective*, ed. Dieter Birnbacher and Edgar Dahl (Dordrecht, the Netherlands: Springer, 2008), 142.

11. *X.Y. v. Health Directorate of the Canton of Zurich, Administrative Court of the Canton of Zurich, and Federal Department of Home Affairs*, 6.3.5.1. (November 3, 2006), trans. Lara Pehar.

12. *Nederlandse Jurisprudentie* 1973, no. 183. The article 40 citation: Dutch Criminal Code, http://www.ejtn.eu/PageFiles/6533/2014%20seminars/Omsenie/WetboekvanStrafrecht_ENG_PV.pdf. Accessed October 4, 2016.

13. *Nederlandse Jurisprudentie* 1987, no. 608.

14. KNMG, "Standpunt inzake Euthanasie [Position on Euthanasia]," *Medisch Contact* 31 (1984): 994–95.

15. The trial: *Tijdschrift voor Gezondheidsrecht* 1993, no. 42. The Supreme Court decision: *Nederlandse Jurisprudentie* 1994, no. 656.

16. The trial: *Tijdschrift voor Gezondheidsrecht* 2001, no. 21. The appeal: *Nederlandse Jurisprudentie* 2003, no. 167.

17. Termination of Life on Request and Assisted Suicide (Review Procedures) Act, Article 2, http://www.eutanasia.ws/documentos/Leyes/Internacional/Holanda Ley 2002.pdf. Accessed October 4, 2016.

18. *Rodriguez v. British Columbia (Attorney General)*, 3 S.C.R. 519 (1993).

19. *Carter v. Canada (Attorney General)*, B.C.S.C. 886 (2012).

20. *Carter v. Canada (Attorney General)*, 1 S.C.R. 331 (2015).

21. An Act to Amend the Criminal Code and to Make Related Amendments to Other Acts (Medical Assistance in Dying), http://www.parl.gc.ca/HousePublications/Publication.aspx?La nguage=E&Mode=1&DocId=8384014. Accessed October 4, 2016.

22. *Washington et al. v. Glucksberg et al.*, 117 S. Ct. 2258 (1997); *Vacco et al. v. Quill et al.*, 117 S. Ct. 2293 (1997).

23. *Gonzales, Attorney General et al. v. Oregon et al.*, 546 U.S. (2006).

24. Washington Death with Dignity Act, http://app.leg.wa.gov/RCW/default.aspx?cite=70.245. Accessed October 5, 2016.

25. *Baxter v. Montana*, MT 449 (2009).

Chapter 6

1. Belgium Act on Euthanasia, Section 3, http://www.ethical-perspectives.be/viewpic.php?LAN=E&TABLE=EP&ID=59. Accessed October 5, 2016.

2. Linda Ganzini, Elizabeth R. Goy, and Steven K. Dobscha, "Why Oregon Patients Request Assisted Death: Family Members' Views," *Journal of General Internal Medicine* 23, no. 2 (2008): 154–57.

3. Linda Ganzini, Elizabeth R. Goy, and Steven K. Dobscha, "Oregonians' Reasons for Requesting Physician Aid in Dying," *Archives of Internal Medicine* 169, no. 5 (2009): 489–92.

4. Scott Y. H. Kim and Raymond G. DeVries, "Euthanasia and Assisted Suicide of Patients with Paychiatric Disorders in the Netherlands, 2011 to 2014," *JAMA Psychiatry* 73, no. 4 (2016): 362–68.

5. *Carter v. Canada (Attorney General)*, 1 S.C.R. 331 (2015).

6. Eva Elizabeth Bolt, et al., "Can Physicians Conceive of Performing Euthanasia in Case of Psychiatric Disease, Dementia or Being Tired of Living?," *Journal of Medical Ethics* 41, no. 8 (2015): 592–98.

7. Marianne C. Snijdewind, et al., "A Study of the First Year of the End-of-Life Clinic for Physician-Assisted Dying in the

Netherlands," *JAMA Internal Medicine* 175, no. 10 (2015): 1633–40; Sigrid Dierickx, et al., "Comparison of the Expression and Granting of Requests for Euthanasia in Belgium in 2007 vs 2013," *JAMA Internal Medicine* 175, no. 10 (2015): 1703–6.

Chapter 7

1. Marcia Angell, "The Quality of Mercy," in *Physician-Assisted Dying: The Case for Palliative Care and Patient Choice*, ed. Timothy E. Quill and Margaret P. Battin (Baltimore and London: Johns Hopkins University Press, 2004), 15–23.
2. Timothy E. Quill, "Principle of Double Effect and End-of-Life Pain Management: Additional Myths and a Limited Role," *Journal of Palliative Medicine* 1, no. 4 (1998): 333–36.
3. Linda Ganzini, Elizabeth R. Goy, and Steven K. Dobscha, "Oregonians' Reasons for Requesting Physician Aid in Dying," *Archives of Internal Medicine* 169, no. 5 (2009): 489–92.
4. R. L. Marquet, et al., "Twenty Five Years of Requests for Euthanasia and Physician Assisted Suicide in Dutch General Practice: Trend Analysis," *British Medical Journal* 327, no. 7408 (2003): 201–2.
5. Linda Ganzini, et al., "Attitudes of Patients with Amyotrophic Lateral Sclerosis and Their Care Givers Toward Assisted Suicide," *New England Journal of Medicine* 339, no. 14 (1998): 967–73.
6. Mario M. Cuomo, "Religious Belief and Public Morality," *New York Review of Books*, October 25, 1984.
7. Andrew Dugan, "In U.S., Support Up for Doctor-Assisted Suicide," Gallup, May 27, 2015, http://www.gallup.com/poll/183425/support-doctor-assisted-suicide.aspx. Accessed June 10, 2016.

Chapter 8

1. Yale Kamisar, "Some Non-Religious Views Against Proposed 'Mercy-Killing' Legislation," *Minnesota Law Review* 42, no. 6 (1958): 969–1042.
2. Yale Kamisar, "Physician-Assisted Suicide: The Last Bridge to Active Voluntary Euthanasia," in *Euthanasia Examined:*

Ethical, Clinical and Legal Perspectives, ed. John Keown (Cambridge: Cambridge University Press, 1995), 225–60.

3. Marianne C. Snijdewind, et al., "A Study of the First Year of the End-of-Life Clinic for Physician-Assisted Dying in the Netherlands," *JAMA Internal Medicine* 175, no. 10 (2015): 1633–40; Sigrid Dierickx, et al., "Comparison of the Expression and Granting of Requests for Euthanasia in Belgium in 2007 vs 2013," *JAMA Internal Medicine* 175, no. 10 (2015): 1703–6.

4. Eva Elizabeth Bolt, et al., "Can Physicians Conceive of Performing Euthanasia in Case of Psychiatric Disease, Dementia or Being Tired of Living?," *Journal of Medical Ethics* 41, no. 8 (2015): 592–98.

5. *Rodriguez v. British Columbia (Attorney General)*, 3 S.C.R. 519, 613 (1993).

6. *Washington et al. v. Glucksberg et al.*, 117 S. Ct. 2258 (1997).

7. Kamisar, "Some Non-Religious Views," 976 (emphasis in original).

8. Ibid., 996.

9. Ibid., 1012.

10. John Keown, *Euthanasia, Ethics and Public Policy: An Argument Against Legalisation* (Cambridge: Cambridge University Press, 2002), 226–27.

11. Katrina George, "A Woman's Choice? The Gendered Risks of Voluntary Euthanasia and Physician-Assisted Suicide," *Medical Law Review* 15, no. 1 (2007): 1–33.

12. Margaret Pabst Battin, et al., "Legal Physician-Assisted Dying in Oregon and the Netherlands: Evidence Concerning the Impact on Patients in 'Vulnerable' Groups," *Journal of Medical Ethics* 33, no. 10 (2007): 594.

13. Ganzini, Goy, and Dobscha, "Oregonians' Reasons for Requesting Physician Aid," 489–92.

14. Battin et al., "Legal Physician-Assisted Dying," 594.

15. Ibid.

16. See the studies summarized in Neil M. Gorsuch, *The Future of Assisted Suicide and Euthanasia* (Princeton, NJ, and Oxford: Princeton University Press, 2006), 126.

17. Dying with Dignity Canada, "Dying with Dignity: Public Perception Survey," https://d3n8a8pro7vhmx.cloudfront.net/dwdcanada/pages/47/attachments/original/1435159000/DWD_IpsosReid2014.pdf?1435159000. Accessed June 10, 2016.

18. Jerome E. Bickenbach, "Disability and Life-Ending Decisions," in *Physician-Assisted Suicide: Expanding the Debate*, ed. Margaret P. Battin, Rosamond Rhodes, and Anita Silvers (New York and London: Routledge, 1998), 123–32.

19. Marilyn Golden and Tyler Zoanni, "Killing Us Softly: The Dangers of Legalizing Assisted Suicide," *Disability and Health Journal* 3, no. 1 (2010): 16–30.

20. Anita Silvers, "Protecting the Innocents from Physician-Assisted Suicide: Disability Discrimination and the Duty to Protect Otherwise Vulnerable Groups," in *Physician-Assisted Suicide: Expanding the Debate*, ed. Margaret P. Battin, Rosamond Rhodes, and Anita Silvers (New York and London: Routledge, 1998), 133–48.

21. Ibid., 137, 146.

22. Charles E. Drum, et al., "The Oregon Death with Dignity Act: Results of a Literature Review and Naturalistic Inquiry," *Disability and Health Journal* 3, no. 1 (2010): 3. The reference to terminal illness is meant to fit within the Oregon criteria for assisted suicide.

23. Ibid., 5. This has been true as well in the Netherlands: Barry Rosenfeld, *Assisted Suicide and the Right to Die: The Interface of Social Science, Public Policy, and Medical Ethics* (Washington, DC: American Psychological Association, 2004), 141.

24. Battin et al., "Legal Physician-Assisted Dying," 594–95.

25. Drum et al., "Oregon Death with Dignity Act," 12.

26. *Carter v. Canada (Attorney General)*, BCSC 886, para 883 (2012).

27. *Carter v. Canada (Attorney General)*, 1 S.C.R. 331, para 117 (2015).

28. H. M. Buiting et al., "Physicians' Labelling of End-of-Life Practices: A Hypothetical Case Study," *Journal of Medical Ethics* 36, no. 1 (2010): 24–29.

29. Leon R. Kass, "Neither for Love Nor Money: Why Doctors Must Not Kill," *Public Interest* 94 (1989): 25–46; Edmund D.

Pellegrino, "Doctors Must Not Kill," *Journal of Clinical Ethics* 3, no. 2 (1992): 95–102.

30. Bernard Baumrin, "Physician, Stay Thy Hand!," in *Physician-Assisted Suicide: Expanding the Debate*, ed. Margaret P. Battin, Rosamond Rhodes, and Anita Silvers (New York and London: Routledge, 1998), 177–81.

31. Tom L. Beauchamp and James F. Childress, *Principles of Biomedical Ethics*, 6th ed. (New York and Oxford: Oxford University Press, 2009).

32. AMA Principles of Medical Ethics, https://download.ama-assn.org/resources/doc/code-medical-ethics/principles-of-medical-ethics-20160627.pdf. Accessed October 6, 2016.

33. Kass, "Neither for Love," 35.

34. Ibid., 35–36.

35. Ilinka Haverkate, et al., "The Emotional Impact on Physicians of Hastening the Death of a Patient," *Medical Journal of Australia* 175, no. 10 (2001): 519–22; K. L. Obstein, G. Kimsma, and T. Chambers, "Practicing Euthanasia: The Perspective of Physicians," *Journal of Clinical Ethics* 15, no. 3 (2004): 223–31.

36. Melinda A. Lee, et al., "Legalizing Assisted Suicide—Views of Physicians in Oregon," *New England Journal of Medicine* 334, no. 5 (1996): 310–15.

37. College des Medecins du Quebec, *Physicians, Appropriate Care and the Debate on Euthanasia: A Reflection* (Montreal, Canada: College des Medecins du Quebec, 2009).

38. George E. Dickinson, et al., "US Physicians' Attitudes Concerning Euthanasia and Physician-Assisted Death: A Systematic Literature Review," *Mortality* 10, no. 1 (2005): 43–52. The range of support for euthanasia was 23%–63%; for assisted suicide 14%–66%.

39. Medscape Ethics Report 2014, Part I: Life, Death, and Pain, http://www.medscape.com/features/slideshow/public/ethics2014-part1?src=ban_wnl_2#2. Accessed June 10, 2016.

40. Jose Pereira, et al., "Assisted Suicide and Euthanasia Should Not Be Practiced in Palliative Care Units," *Journal of Palliative Medicine* 11, no. 8 (2008): 1074–76.

41. World Health Organization, *Palliative Care*, Fact Sheet no. 402, http://www.who.int/mediacentre/factsheets/fs402/en/. Accessed October 8, 2016.

42. Jan L. Bernheim, et al., "Development of Palliative Care and Legalisation of Euthanasia: Antagonism or Synergy?," *British Medical Journal* 336, no. 7649 (2008): 864–67.

43. American Academy of Hospice and Palliative Medicine, "Statement on Physician-Assisted Dying," http://aahpm.org/positions/pad. Accessed October 8, 2016.

44. Personal communication from Ann Jackson, CEO of the Oregon Hospice Association, January 18, 2007.

45. Timothy E. Quill, "Principle of Double Effect and End-of-Life Pain Management: Additional Myths and a Limited Role," *Journal of Palliative Medicine* 1, no. 4 (1998): 333–36.

46. Michael B. Gill, "Is the Legalization of Physician-Assisted Suicide Compatible with Good End-of-Life Care?," *Journal of Applied Philosophy* 26, no. 1 (2009): 38–39.

47. For example, Keown, *Euthanasia, Ethics*, 111.

48. John Griffiths, Heleen Weyers, and Maurice Adams, *Euthanasia and Law in Europe* (Oxford and Portland, OR: Hart Publishing, 2008), 18.

49. Economist Intelligence Unit, "The 2015 Quality of Death Index: Ranking Palliative Care Across the World," https://www.eiuperspectives.economist.com/sites/default/files/2015%20EIU%20Quality%20of%20Death%20Index%20Oct%2029%20FINAL.pdf. Accessed June 10, 2016. Belgium ranked fifth in the same index.

50. Angell, "Quality of Mercy," 20–21.

51. J. L. Bernat, B. Gert, and R. P. Mogielnicki, "Patient Refusal of Hydration and Nutrition—An Alternative to Physician-Assisted Suicide or Voluntary Active Euthanasia," *Archives of Internal Medicine* 153, no. 24 (1993): 2723–28.

52. Dan W. Brock, "Physician-Assisted Suicide as a Last-Resort Option at the End of Life," in *Physician-Assisted Dying: The Case for Palliative Care and Patient Choice*, ed. Timothy E. Quill and Margaret P. Battin (Baltimore and London: Johns Hopkins University Press, 2004), 132.

Chapter 9

1. *In re Quinlan*, 355 A.2d 647 (N.J., 1976).
2. *Cruzan v. Director, Missouri Department of Health*, 497 U.S. 261 (1990).
3. Rebecca Dresser, "Life, Death, and Incompetent Patients: Conceptual Infirmities and Hidden Values in the Law," *Arizona Law Review* 28, no. 3 (1986): 373–405; Rebecca Dresser, "Precommitment: A Misguided Strategy for Securing Death with Dignity," *Texas Law Review* 81, no. 7 (2003): 1823–47.
4. Kathrine Bendtsen, "Communicating with the Minimally Conscious: Ethical Implications in End-of-Life Care," *AJOB Neuroscience* 4, no. 1 (2013): 46–51.
5. Termination of Life on Request and Assisted Suicide (Review Procedures) Act, Article 2, http://www.eutanasia.ws/documentos/Leyes/Internacional/Holanda Ley 2002.pdf. Accessed October 4, 2016.
6. Belgium Act on Euthanasia, Section 4, http://www.ethical-perspectives.be/viewpic.php?LAN=E&TABLE=EP&ID=59. Accessed October 5, 2016.
7. Ronald Dworkin, *Life's Dominion: An Argument About Abortion, Euthanasia, and Individual Freedom* (New York: Random House, 1993), 220–21.
8. Rebecca Dresser, "Dworkin on Dementia: Elegant Theory, Questionable Policy," *Hastings Center Report* 25, no. 6 (1995): 36.
9. Dresser, "Precommitment," 1840.
10. Caroline Schnakers, et al., "Diagnostic Accuracy of the Vegetative and Minimally Conscious State: Clinical Consensus Versus Standardized Neurobehavioral Assessment," *BMC Neurology* 9, no. 35 (2009): 35.
11. Jim Stone, "Pascal's Wager and the Persistent Vegetative State," *Bioethics* 21, no. 2 (2007): 84–92.
12. Martin M. Monti, et al., "Willful Modulation of Brain Activity in Disorders of Consciousness," *New England Journal of Medicine* 362 (2010): 579–89.

13. Agnieszka Jaworska, "Respecting the Margins of Agency: Alzheimer's Patients and the Capacity to Value," *Philosophy & Public Affairs* 28, no. 2 (1999): 105–38.

14. *Superintendent of Belchertown State School v. Saikewicz*, 370 N.E.2d 417 (Mass., 1977).

15. Bryson Brown, "Robert Latimer's Choice," in *The Price of Compassion: Assisted Suicide and Euthanasia in Canada and the United States*, ed. Michael Stingl (Peterborough, Canada: Broadview Press, 2010), 161–86.

16. *R. v. Latimer*, 1 S.C.R. 3 (2001).

17. For three of these cases, see Helga Kuhse and Peter Singer, *Should the Baby Live? The Problem of Handicapped Infants* (Oxford: Oxford University Press, 1985), chs. 1 and 4.

18. Ibid., 146ff. See also James R. Rodrigue, Sam B. Morgan, and Gary Geffken, "Families of Autistic Children: Psychological Functioning of Mothers," *Journal of Clinical Child Psychology* 19, no. 4 (1990): 371–79; M. Cuskelly and P. Gunn, "Maternal Reports of Behavior of Siblings of Children with Down Syndrome," *American Journal on Mental Retardation* 97, no. 5 (1993): 521–29.

19. Kuhse and Singer, *Should the Baby Live?*, ch. 3.

20. John Lorber, "Ethical Problems in the Management of Myelomeningocele and Hydrocephalus," *Journal of the Royal College of Physicians* 10, no. 1 (1975): 47–60.

21. Kuhse and Singer, *Should the Baby Live?*, 57.

22. See, for instance, Nuffield Council on Bioethics, *Critical Care Decisions in Fetal and Neonatal Medicine: Ethical Issues* (London: Nuffield Council on Bioethics, 2006).

23. Eduard Verhagen and Pieter J. J. Sauer, "The Groningen Protocol: Euthanasia in Severely Ill Newborns," *New England Journal of Medicine* 352, no. 10 (2005): 959–62.

24. Alexander A. Kon, "Neonatal Euthanasia Is Unsupportable: The Groningen Protocol Should Be Abandoned," *Theoretical Medicine and Bioethics* 28, no. 5 (2007): 457 (emphasis in original).

Chapter 10

1. Margaret Pabst Battin, *Ending Life: Ethics and the Way We Die* (Oxford: Oxford University Press, 2005), 63–66.
2. Timothy E. Quill, "Death and Dignity—A Case of Individualized Decision Making," *New England Journal of Medicine* 324, no. 10 (1991): 691–94.
3. *Baxter v. Montana*, MT 449 (2009).
4. Crown Prosecution Service, "Policy for Prosecutors in Respect of Cases of Encouraging or Assisting Suicide," last modified October 2014, http://www.cps.gov.uk/publications/prosecution/assisted_suicide_policy.html. Accessed October 8, 2016.

BIBLIOGRAPHY

Ad Hoc Committee of the Harvard Medical School. "A Definition of Irreversible Coma." *Journal of the American Medical Association* 205, no. 6 (1968): 337–40.

American Academy of Hospice and Palliative Medicine. "Statement on Physician-Assisted Dying." http://aahpm.org/positions/pad. Accessed October 8, 2016.

Angell, Marcia. "The Quality of Mercy." In *Physician-Assisted Dying: The Case for Palliative Care and Patient Choice*, edited by Timothy E. Quill and Margaret P. Battin, 15–23. Baltimore: Johns Hopkins University Press, 2004.

Angus, Floyd, and Robert Burakoff. "The Percutaneous Endoscopic Gastrostomy Tube: Medical and Ethical Issues in Placement." *American Journal of Gastroenterology* 98, no. 2 (2003): 272–77.

Baezner-Sailer, Elke M. "Physician-Assisted Suicide in Switzerland: A Personal Report." In *Giving Death a Helping Hand: Physician-Assisted Suicide and Public Policy, an International Perspective*, edited by Dieter Birnbacher and Edgar Dahl, 141–48. Dordrecht, the Netherlands: Springer, 2008.

Battin, Margaret Pabst. *Ending Life: Ethics and the Way We Die*. Oxford: Oxford University Press, 2005.

Battin, Margaret Pabst, Agnes van der Heide, Linda Ganzini, Gerrit van der Wal, and Bregje D. Onwuteaka-Philipsen. "Legal Physician-Assisted Dying in Oregon and the Netherlands:

Evidence Concerning the Impact on Patients in 'Vulnerable' Groups." *Journal of Medical Ethics* 33, no. 10 (2007): 591–97.

Baumrin, Bernard. "Physician, Stay Thy Hand!" In *Physician-Assisted Suicide: Expanding the Debate*, edited by Margaret P. Battin, Rosamond Rhodes, and Anita Silvers, 177–81. New York and London: Routledge, 1998.

Beauchamp, Tom L., and James F. Childress. *Principles of Biomedical Ethics*. 6th ed. New York and Oxford: Oxford University Press, 2009.

Bendtsen, Kathrine. "Communicating with the Minimally Conscious: Ethical Implications in End-of-Life Care." *AJOB Neuroscience* 4, no. 1 (2013): 46–51.

Bernat, J. L., B. Gert, and R. P. Mogielnicki. "Patient Refusal of Hydration and Nutrition—An Alternative to Physician-Assisted Suicide or Voluntary Active Euthanasia." *Archives of Internal Medicine* 153, no. 24 (1993): 2723–31.

Bernheim, Jan L., Reginald Deschepper, Wim Distelmans, Arsène Mullie, Johan Bilsen, and Luc Deliens. "Development of Palliative Care and Legalisation of Euthanasia: Antagonism or Synergy?" *British Medical Journal* 336, no. 7649 (2008): 864–67.

Bickenbach, Jerome E. "Disability and Life-Ending Decisions." In *Physician-Assisted Suicide: Expanding the Debate*, edited by Margaret P. Battin, Rosamond Rhodes, and Anita Silvers, 123–32. New York and London: Routledge, 1998.

Bolt, Eva Elizabeth, Marianne C. Snijdewind, Dick L. Willems, Agnes van der Heide, and Bregje D. Onwuteaka-Philipsen. "Can Physicians Conceive of Performing Euthanasia in Case of Psychiatric Disease, Dementia or Being Tired of Living?" *Journal of Medical Ethics* 41, no. 8 (2015): 592–98.

Brock, Dan W. "Physician-Assisted Suicide as a Last-Resort Option at the End of Life." In *Physician-Assisted Dying: The Case for Palliative Care and Patient Choice*, edited by Timothy E. Quill and Margaret P. Battin, 130–49. Baltimore: Johns Hopkins University Press, 2004.

Brown, Bryson. "Robert Latimer's Choice." In *The Price of Compassion: Assisted Suicide and Euthanasia in Canada and the*

United States, edited by Michael Stingl, 161–86. Peterborough, Canada: Broadview Press, 2010.

Buchanan, Allen, and Dan W. Brock. *Deciding for Others: The Ethics of Surrogate Decision Making*. Cambridge: Cambridge University Press, 1989.

Buiting, H. M., A. van der Heide, B. D. Onwuteaka-Philipsen, M. L. Rurup, J. A. C. Rietjens, G. Borsboom, P. J. van der Maas, and J. J. M. van Delden. "Physicians' Labelling of End-of-Life Practices: A Hypothetical Case Study." *Journal of Medical Ethics* 36, no. 1 (2010): 24–29.

Cohen-Almagor, Raphael. *Euthanasia in the Netherlands: The Policy and Practice of Mercy Killing*. Dordrecht, the Netherlands: Kluwer Academic, 2004.

College des Medecins du Quebec. *Physicians, Appropriate Care and the Debate on Euthanasia: A Reflection*. Montreal, Canada: College des Medecins du Quebec, 2009.

Crown Prosecution Service. "Policy for Prosecutors in Respect of Cases of Encouraging or Assisting Suicide." Last modified October 2014. http://www.cps.gov.uk/publications/prosecution/assisted_suicide_policy.html. Accessed October 8, 2016.

Cuomo, Mario M. "Religious Belief and Public Morality." *New York Review of Books*, October 25, 1984.

Cuskelly, M., and P. Gunn. "Maternal Reports of Behavior of Siblings of Children with Down Syndrome." *American Journal on Mental Retardation* 97, no. 5 (1993): 521–29.

Dickinson, George E., David Clark, Michelle Winslow, and Rachael Marples. "US Physicians' Attitudes Concerning Euthanasia and Physician-Assisted Death: A Systematic Literature Review." *Mortality* 10, no. 1 (2005): 43–52.

Dierickx, Sigrid, Luc Deliens, Joachim Cohen, and Kenneth Chambaere. "Comparison of the Expression and Granting of Requests for Euthanasia in Belgium in 2007 vs 2013." *JAMA Internal Medicine* 175, no. 10 (2015): 1703–6.

Donagan, Alan. *The Theory of Morality*. Chicago: University of Chicago Press, 1977.

Dresser, Rebecca. "Dworkin on Dementia: Elegant Theory, Questionable Policy." *Hastings Center Report* 25, no. 6 (1995): 32–38.

———. "Life, Death, and Incompetent Patients: Conceptual Infirmities and Hidden Values in the Law." *Arizona Law Review* 28, no. 3 (1986): 373–406.

———. "Precommitment: A Misguided Strategy for Securing Death with Dignity." *Texas Law Review* 81, no. 7 (2003): 1823–48.

Drum, Charles E., Glen White, Genia Taitano, and Willi Horner-Johnson. "The Oregon Death with Dignity Act: Results of a Literature Review and Naturalistic Inquiry." *Disability and Health Journal* 3, no. 1 (2010): 3–15.

Dugan, Andrew. "In U.S., Support Up for Doctor-Assisted Suicide." Gallup, May 27, 2015. http://www.gallup.com/poll/183425/support-doctor-assisted-suicide.aspx. Accessed June 10, 2016.

Dutch Criminal Code. http://www.ejtn.eu/PageFiles/6533/2014%20seminars/Omsenie/WetboekvanStrafrecht_ENG_PV.pdf. Accessed October 4, 2016.

Dworkin, Ronald. *Life's Dominion: An Argument About Abortion, Euthanasia, and Individual Freedom*. New York: Random House, 1993.

Dying with Dignity Canada. "Dying with Dignity: Public Perception Survey." https://d3n8a8pro7vhmx.cloudfront.net/dwdcanada/pages/47/attachments/original/1435159000/DWD_IpsosReid2014.pdf?1435159000. Accessed June 10, 2016.

Economist Intelligence Unit. "The 2015 Quality of Death Index: Ranking Palliative Care Across the World." https://www.eiuperspectives.economist.com/sites/default/files/2015%20EIU%20Quality%20of%20Death%20Index%20Oct%2029%20FINAL.pdf. Accessed June 10, 2016.

Finnis, John. "A Philosophical Case Against Euthanasia." In *Euthanasia Examined: Ethical, Clinical and Legal Perspectives*, edited by John Keown, 23–35. Cambridge: Cambridge University Press, 1995.

———. *Natural Law and Natural Rights*. Oxford: Clarendon Press, 1980.

Fohr, Susan Anderson. "The Double Effect of Pain Medication: Separating Myth from Reality." *Journal of Palliative Medicine* 1, no. 4 (1998): 315–28.

Ganzini, Linda, Elizabeth R. Goy, and Steven K. Dobscha. "Oregonians' Reasons for Requesting Physician Aid in Dying." *Archives of Internal Medicine* 169, no. 5 (2009): 489–92.

———. "Why Oregon Patients Request Assisted Death: Family Members' Views." *Journal of General Internal Medicine* 23, no. 2 (2008): 154–7.

Ganzini, Linda, Wendy S. Johnston, Bentson H. McFarland, Susan W. Tolle, and Melinda A. Lee. "Attitudes of Patients with Amyotrophic Lateral Sclerosis and Their Care Givers Toward Assisted Suicide." *New England Journal of Medicine* 339, no. 14 (1998): 967–73.

Ganzini, Linda, Heidi D. Nelson, Melinda A. Lee, Dale F. Kraemer, Terri Schmidt, and Terri A. Delorit. "Oregon Physicians' Attitudes About and Experiences with End-of-Life Care Since the Passage of the Oregon Death with Dignity Act." *Journal of the American Medical Association* 285, no. 18 (2001): 2363–69.

Gawandi, Atul. *Being Mortal: Medicine and What Matters in the End.* New York: Metropolitan Books, 2014.

Gaylin, Willard, Leon R. Kass, Edmund D. Pellegrino, and Mark M. Siegler. "Doctors Must Not Kill." *Journal of the American Medical Association* 259, no. 14 (1988): 2139–40.

George, Katrina. "A Woman's Choice? The Gendered Risks of Voluntary Euthanasia and Physician-Assisted Suicide." *Medical Law Review* 15, no. 1 (2007): 1–33.

Gill, Michael B. "Is the Legalization of Physician-Assisted Suicide Compatible with Good End-of-Life Care?" *Journal of Applied Philosophy* 26, no. 1 (2009): 27–45.

Glover, Jonathan. *Causing Death and Saving Lives.* Harmondsworth, UK: Penguin Books, 1977.

Golden, Marilyn, and Tyler Zoanni. "Killing Us Softly: The Dangers of Legalizing Assisted Suicide." *Disability and Health Journal* 3, no. 1 (2010): 16–30.

Gorsuch, Neil M. *The Future of Assisted Suicide and Euthanasia*. Princeton, NJ, and Oxford: Princeton University Press, 2006.

Griffiths, John, Heleen Weyers, and Maurice Adams. *Euthanasia and Law in Europe*. Oxford and Portland, OR: Hart Publishing, 2008.

Haverkate, Ilinka, Agnes van der Heide, Bregje D. Onwuteaka-Philipsen, Paul J. van der Maas, and Gerrit van der Wal. "The Emotional Impact on Physicians of Hastening the Death of a Patient." *Medical Journal of Australia* 175, no. 10 (2001): 519–22.

Jaworska, Agnieszka. "Respecting the Margins of Agency: Alzheimer's Patients and the Capacity to Value." *Philosophy & Public Affairs* 28, no. 2 (1999): 105–38.

Kamisar, Yale. "Physician-Assisted Suicide: The Last Bridge to Active Voluntary Euthanasia." In *Euthanasia Examined: Ethical, Clinical and Legal Perspectives*, edited by John Keown, 225–60. Cambridge: Cambridge University Press, 1995.

———. "Some Non-Religious Views Against Proposed 'Mercy-Killing' Legislation." *Minnesota Law Review* 42, no. 6 (1958): 969–1042.

Kass, Leon R. "Neither for Love Nor Money: Why Doctors Must Not Kill." *Public Interest* 94 (1989): 25–46.

Keown, John. *Euthanasia, Ethics and Public Policy: An Argument Against Legalisation*. Cambridge: Cambridge University Press, 2002.

Kim, Scott Y. H., Raymond G. DeVries, and John R. Peteet. "Euthanasia and Assisted Suicide of Patients with Psychiatric Disorders in the Netherlands 2011 to 2014." *JAMA Psychiatry* 73, no. 4 (2016): 362–68.

KNMG. "Standpunt inzake Euthanasie [Position on Euthanasia]." *Medisch Contact* 31 (1984): 990–97.

Kon, Alexander A. "Neonatal Euthanasia Is Unsupportable: The Groningen Protocol Should Be Abandoned." *Theoretical Medicine and Bioethics* 28, no. 5 (2007): 453–63.

Kuhse, Helga, and Peter Singer. *Should the Baby Live? The Problem of Handicapped Infants*. Oxford: Oxford University Press, 1985.

Lee, Melinda A., Heidi D. Nelson, Virginia P. Tilden, Linda Ganzini, Terri A. Schmidt, and Susan Tolle. "Legalizing Assisted Suicide—Views of Physicians in Oregon." *New England Journal of Medicine* 334, no. 5 (1996): 310–15.

Lorber, John. "Ethical Problems in the Management of Myelomeningocele and Hydrocephalus." *Journal of the Royal College of Physicians* 10, no. 1 (1975): 47–60.

Lucretius. "On the Nature of Things." In *The Stoic and Epicurean Philosophers: The Complete Extant Writings of Epicurus, Epictetus, Lucretius, Marcus Aurelius,* edited by Whitney J. Oates, 69–219. New York: Modern Library, 1940.

Maltoni, M., E. Pittureri, E. Scarpi, L. Piccinini, F. Martini, P. Turci, L. Montanari, O. Nanni, and D. Amadori. "Palliative Sedation Therapy Does Not Hasten Death: Results from a Prospective Multicenter Study." *Annals of Oncology* 20, no. 7 (2009): 1163–69.

Marquet, R. L., A. Bartelds, G. J. Visser, P. Spreeuwenberg, and L. Peters. "Twenty Five Years of Requests for Euthanasia and Physician Assisted Suicide in Dutch General Practice: Trend Analysis." *British Medical Journal* 327, no. 7408 (2003): 201–2.

Monti, Martin M., Audrey Vanhaudenhuyse, Martin R. Coleman, Melanie Boly, John D. Pickard, Luaba Tshibanda, Adrian M. Owen, and Steven Laureys. "Willful Modulation of Brain Activity in Disorders of Consciousness." *New England Journal of Medicine* 362, no. 7 (2010): 579–89.

Nuffield Council on Bioethics. *Critical Care Decisions in Fetal and Neonatal Medicine: Ethical Issues.* London: Nuffield Council on Bioethics, 2006.

Nuremberg Tribunal. "The Nuremberg Code." In *Doctors of Infamy: The Story of the Nazi Medical Crimes,* edited by A. Mitscherlich and F. Mielke, xxiii–xxv. New York: Schuman, 1947.

Obstein, K. L., G. Kimsma, and T. Chambers. "Practicing Euthanasia: The Perspective of Physicians." *Journal of Clinical Ethics* 15, no. 3 (2004): 223–31.

Pellegrino, Edmund D. "Doctors Must Not Kill." *Journal of Clinical Ethics* 3, no. 2 (1992): 95–102.

Pereira, Jose, Dominique Anwar, Gerard Pralong, Josianne Pralong, Claudia Mazzocato, and Jean-Michel Bigler. "Assisted Suicide and Euthanasia Should Not Be Practiced in Palliative Care Units." *Journal of Palliative Medicine* 11, no. 8 (2008): 1074–76.

Quill, Timothy E. "Death and Dignity—A Case of Individualized Decision Making." *New England Journal of Medicine* 324, no. 10 (1991): 691–94.

———. "Principle of Double Effect and End-of-Life Pain Management: Additional Myths and a Limited Role." *Journal of Palliative Medicine* 1, no. 4 (1998): 333–36.

Rodrigue, James R., Sam B. Morgan, and Gary Geffken. "Families of Autistic Children: Psychological Functioning of Mothers." *Journal of Clinical Child Psychology* 19, no. 4 (1990): 371–79.

Rosenfeld, Barry. *Assisted Suicide and the Right to Die: The Interface of Social Science, Public Policy, and Medical Ethics.* Washington, DC: American Psychological Association, 2004.

Rosner, Fred. "Why Nutrition and Hydration Should Not Be Withheld from Patients." *Chest* 104, no. 6 (1993): 1892–96.

Schnakers, Caroline, Audrey Vanhaudenhuyse, Joseph Giacino, Manfredi Ventura, Melanie Boly, Steve Majerus, Gustave Moonen, and Steven Laureys. "Diagnostic Accuracy of the Vegetative and Minimally Conscious State: Clinical Consensus Versus Standardized Neurobehavioral Assessment." *BMC Neurology* 9, no. 35 (2009). DOI: 10.1186/1471-2377-9-35.

Siegler, M., and A. Weisbard. "Against the Emerging Stream: Should Fluids and Nutritional Support Be Discontinued?" *Archives of Internal Medicine* 145, no. 1 (1985): 129–31.

Silvers, Anita. "Protecting the Innocents from Physician-Assisted Suicide: Disability Discrimination and the Duty to Protect Otherwise Vulnerable Groups." In *Physician-Assisted Suicide: Expanding the Debate*, edited by Margaret P. Battin, Rosamond Rhodes, and Anita Silvers, 133–48. New York and London: Routledge, 1998.

Snijdewind, Marianne C., Dick L. Willems, Luc Deliens, Bregje D. Onwuteaka-Philipsen, and Kenneth Chambaere. "A Study of the First Year of the End-of-Life Clinic for Physician-Assisted Dying in the Netherlands." *JAMA Internal Medicine* 175, no. 10 (2015): 1633–40.

Stone, Jim. "Pascal's Wager and the Persistent Vegetative State." *Bioethics* 21, no. 2 (2007): 84–92.

Stanford School of Medicine. "Where Do Americans Die?" https://palliative.stanford.edu/home-hospice-home-care-of-the-dying-patient/where-do-americans-die/. Accessed June 10, 2016.

Sumner, L. W. *Assisted Death: A Study in Ethics and Law.* Oxford: Oxford University Press, 2011.

Swiss National Advisory Commission for Biomedical Ethics (NEK-CNE). *Assisted Suicide: Opinion No. 9/2005.* Bern: NEK-CNE, 2005.

Swiss Penal Code [*Schweitzerisches Strafgesetzbuch*]. https://www.admin.ch/opc/de/classified-compilation/19370083/index.html. Accessed October 4, 2016.

Verhagen, Eduard, and Pieter J. J. Sauer. "The Groningen Protocol: Euthanasia in Severely Ill Newborns." *New England Journal of Medicine* 352, no. 10 (2005): 959–62.

World Health Organization. *Palliative Care.* Fact Sheet no. 402. http://www.who.int/mediacentre/factsheets/fs402/en/. Accessed October 8, 2016.

Ziegler, Stephen J., and Georg Bosshard. "Role of Non-Governmental Organisations in Physician Assisted Suicide." *British Medical Journal* 334, no. 7588 (2007): 295–98.

INDEX

Printed in the USA/Agawam, MA
January 24, 2018

668384.007